PRAISE FOR EMOTIONAL READINESS

Change is accelerating exponentially. That's just a fact. But it means that any child who does not master the complex skill of empathy will not be able to navigate an ever more complex and rapidly shifting human environment. Terrie Rose, a very leading social entrepreneur, is opening this critical door to every child, including those in very high-risk, high-violence situations. She sees their potential and assets. She sees the world from the baby's point of view.

Bill Drayton, CEO, Ashoka: Innovators for the Public

Dr. Terrie Rose is one of our nation's leading child psychologists and innovators. In this book, Dr. Rose makes a persuasive case for raising the awareness and understanding of the social and emotional needs of children in the very earliest years of development. While as a society we have created a high awareness of our children's physical needs and developed systems to help our children start school physically healthy and ready to learn, Dr. Rose argues that we are seriously behind in ensuring the social and emotional readiness of our children. Dr. Rose's book, however, is much more than a compelling insight into the problem; it is also a call to action. It is a call to parents to be just as sensitive to social and emotional infections as they are to ear infections. It is a call to pediatricians to routinely use the tools that child psychologists have developed to identify and treat social and emotional problems. (Like ear infections, if not treated in the early years, these problems have serious long-term consequences to a child's health and well-being.) And finally, because research has shown that there is no better public investment than the health and well being of our children, it is a call to policy makers to significantly increase funding to address social and emotional well-being, especially for our most vulnerable children. A must read for public officials responsible for our children's success, as well as for caregivers.

Arthur J. Rolnick, senior fellow and co-director of the Human Capital Research Collaborative, Hubert H. Humphrey School of Public Affairs, University of Minnesota

D0109836

As a pediatrician and child advocate, I am delighted that Dr. Rose has given us this enjoyable, tremendously informative, and unique read on early childhood social, emotional and mental health development. I know I will recommend it to friends, family, and patients.

George L. Askew, MD, FAAP, founder and former executive director, Docs For Tots and former deputy CEO, Voices for America's Children

Terrie Rose says it loud and clear: What every baby and family needs to assure optimal health and growth are nurturing relationships within caring communities.

In her wonderful new book, Emotional Readiness, Dr. Rose reflects on her own beginnings as a mother, sometimes lonely, often overwhelmed and in need of guidance and support. Out of deeply personal experiences, she created Baby's Space, a responsive and caring environment that extends relationship support to the most vulnerable families. She invites readers to consider early care from the baby's point of view, focusing on practical approaches to responsive care. Easy to read, inspiring and practical, this book should be in the hands of every infant and early childhood service provider.

Deborah J. Weatherston, PhD, IMH-E® (IV), executive director, Michigan Association for Infant Mental Health and editor, Perspectives in Infant Mental Health, World Association for IMH

Preparing children to be "ready" for school—and success in life as well as academics—demands a greater thoughtfulness than what we see in current public policy. Over the last decade, Terrie Rose has shared her stories and her knowledge of babies with the Minnesota Head Start community. We have learned to recognize mental health in young children through her illustrations and support of reliable techniques for screening, diagnosis and treatment.

In Emotional Readiness, Dr. Rose brings together research on early childhood that forces us to think differently about how we foster the growth and development of young children. She sees child development through the baby's point of view and helps adults understand how important it is for them to create the nurturing relationships that support children's emotional and academic success. Emotional Readiness calls parents, professionals and policymakers to intervene early in the lives of young children and their families.

The book is a valuable contribution to early childhood and the discussion of school readiness. We share Dr. Rose's vision of communities that build a network of support for families and ask frequently, "How is the baby?"

Gayle Kelly, executive director, Minnesota Head Start Association, Inc.

Terrie Rose has written about emotional readiness for our youngsters from seven different perspectives, beginning with her first comprehension of what young, single working mothers faced when federal welfare law was changed in the '90s to require women to work if they sought welfare eligibility.

What makes this book especially useful for practioners, policymakers and parents are the descriptions of what works from each perspective, beginning with prenatal readiness and ending with community readiness. These perspectives emphasize outcomes for the child and provide guidance on what works and what to do if problems arise. Sometimes the problems are serious and require professional intervention, other times some parental initiative is sufficient to address the problem.

Terrie Rose's unique approach to working with children was—and is—an important addition for the residents of the urban Indian community in which it was founded. But anyone who cares about young children and parents will benefit from reading this book—so will any community organizer who seeks a deeper understanding of how to become more effective in working with families under financial stress.

Don Fraser, early childhood education advocate, former U.S. Representative and former mayor of Minneapolis

Dr. Terrie Rose brings together brain science, research and on-the-rug experience to show how early experiences shape young children, influencing their vulnerabilities, resilience, and ability to build healthy relationships with others. Emotional Readiness is a richly detailed and practical guide to understanding early childhood development, with direct action implications for pediatricians, educators, community leaders, parents and policymakers.

David Bornstein, Writer, New York Times Fixes Column, Co-founder, Solutions Journalism Network

Emotional Readiness

How Early Experience and Mental Health
Predict School Success

Terrie Rose, PhD

Copyright © 2013 Terrie Rose

ISBN10:1489557148
ISBN-13:978-1489557148

Book design by Rebecca Rose & Ryan Scheife

DEDICATION

This book is dedicated to Don Fraser and Dr. Esther Wattenberg, whose commitment to children and families is inspirational.

CONTENTS

ACKNOWLEDGMENTS

This book would not have been possible without the love, support, and partnership of family, friends, colleagues and the board, staff, children and families of the Baby's Space community.

I would like to give special appreciation for the unwavering support of my husband and family. Larry, Elizabeth, Rebecca, Max, Francene and Sheldon thank you for sharing this journey with me and of teaching me the meaning of secure, responsive and sensitive relationships.

Deb Lund is an extraordinary person whose compassion and commitment brings joy to so many and skillfully guides the work at Baby's Space.

Baby's Space was born with the support of Mary and Jeff Werbalowsky. I could not have achieved the mission without their consistent leadership as generous and engaged philanthropists.

I remain grateful to all of those individuals and foundations that have contributed to Baby's Space's abilities to provide high-quality, consistent direct services.

To the organizations and individuals of Ashoka and Social Venture Partners who provided vital recognition, opportunities for learning, and support as a social entrepreneur, I am forever beholden.

My gratitude extends to the many dedicated advisors and colleagues at the University of Minnesota who nurtured my understanding of research and practice in the fields of attachment, mental health, child development and adversity.

A number of people contributed to the editing process. The expertise and guidance of Dr. Nancy Wagner and Linda Picone helped me find my voice and confidence as a writer. I am particularly grateful for Emily Fenichel, may she rest in peace, who was the first to encourage me to write a book.

I thank all of my colleagues who work side-by-side-in policy, practice, research and training to enhance the opportunities for success of young children and families.

Finally, I am especially appreciative for the children, families and staff who allow me to walk the path with them.

1

"Baby's Space has really helped me love being a parent."

BABY'S SPACE

Responsive, consistent, and loving relationships with adults are essential to every step of a child's development. And, as we all know, the first and most influential adult is the parent. This primary relationship provides the foundation by which a child learns about herself and her connections with others. Everyday experiences cultivate the child's ability to express empathy, regulate emotions, and engage in learning. Life's successes and challenges are interpreted through the lessons of this central relationships.

For parents, this role is both delightful and daunting. Parenting is enchanting when a baby follows a regular schedule, a toddler is cooperative, and a preschooler plays with a friend. However, the endless demands of being a responsive parent and the monotonous tasks of caregiving can challenge our best intentions. All of us want to be good parents but many of us may not know where to start or who to turn to when parenting becomes complicated or hits unexpected challenges. For those living with poverty and violence, or for those struggling with addiction, limited education and lack of good role models, caring for a child competes with an crushing number of challenges.

Baby's Space was designed out of compassion for the complications of parenting, the knowledge of the critical function of the parent-child relationship, and the deep belief that if we take the baby's point of view, we can better prepare our children for the future. Baby's Space sits at the epicenter of the neighborhood, remaining firmly committed to sustaining the everyday experiences that support emotional readiness and school success.

"The days are long, the years are short."

LEARNING TO BE A PARENT

Just after our second daughter turned 1, when we felt as if we finally had a handle on parenting two young children, we flew to my in-laws for Thanksgiving weekend, planning to spend three days with doting grandparents who would help us entertain two active toddlers. During that visit, my husband and I discovered that our very sensible plan to wait to have a third child had been thwarted. Within the next year, we became parents again.

Three children in just three years.

Our earth was moving and we were relatively unprepared for the unrelenting waves of expectations and exhaustion that were about to hit. We were unprepared for the sheer output of energy necessary to live up to our expectations of how to parent three closely spaced children.

I remember one beautiful day in October, a day straight out of a fall spread in Martha Stewart Living, I was driving my three children, aged 3, 1½ and 4 months, from the grocery store to the pumpkin patch.

I was far from the put-together young mother of the magazine with a cream-colored cable knit sweater, perfect hair and an unwavering smile. Dressed in an old college sweatshirt with a hole in the collar and yogurt on the shoulder, I pulled my car into the farm's dirt parking lot while tears flowed down my cheeks. My image of a picture-perfect day out with my kids, running an errand and picking out pumpkins, was completely dissolving as the realities of sleep deprivation, the unrelenting neediness of three small children and my own limitations crashed in on me.

I joined parent education classes, not telling anyone about my background in psychology and early childhood education. I wanted to chat and have coffee with the other mothers while my children were well cared for in the early education classroom. When reunited for parent-child interaction time, I was not the most cooperative participant, preferring to let my children play while I continued conversations with the other mothers. From my point of view, this was my relief from the constant demands of motherhood.

> One winter day, when everything outside was covered in snow and the temperature was below zero, we were housebound for the third day in a row. I was sleep-deprived and cranky. My three little ones were full of energy and each of them needed my full attention. My patience was wearing thin and I began to doubt that I could make it through the day without losing my cool. Just hearing the word "mom" made my skin crawl. In an effort to preserve my sanity, I launched a small, yet ultimately satisfying, personal mutiny. I announced to my children:

> "Sam. You have to call me Sam. For today, I am not answering to 'Mom.' Sam, I am."

> After a few unsuccessful attempts to get my attention, my children quickly switched to asking "Sam" for what they needed. For that day, I was able to be a better parent as Sam than I was able to be as "Mom." The day I was Sam is a longstanding part of our family lore now. My children remember its silliness fondly, but I remember it with gratitude that I could use comedy to rescue my sanity and parenting.

Self-reflection, humor and the support of my husband, friends and family carried me through unexpected moments and emotions during my children's early years and allowed me to respond with objectivity rather than self-reproach and criticism. I was lucky to have a PhD in child psychology and lots of practical experience as a teacher and therapist. I remember once, as I was restraining my thrashing

3-year-old son on my lap, he finally looked up at me and said, "Where you learn that?" I had definitely learned a few handy tricks.

"No longer are mothers subsidized to stay home to raise their babies."

With A New Understanding of Parenting

When my youngest was about to enter kindergarten, the STEEP™ home-visiting research project I'd been working on was done, but services continued for the high-risk families studied.

As I was leaving the clinic to head home to our three young children, I watched as Sandra, a young mother who was in our parenting program tried to convince her 3-year-old to walk two blocks to catch the bus while she pushed a double stroller over the snow covered sidewalks. I knew how futile it felt to be dependent on the cooperation of a 3-year-old and the physical exhaustion and worry of getting all three children to the stop and then onto the bus. It was hard enough for me to get through the grocery store where the lower level of the cart was built like a racecar and the bakery handed out free cookies.

I could hardly imagine her daily struggles to remain sober, care for her children while living in a neighborhood with so few resources. After all, I had a home with an attached garage, a caring spouse and a community of support and I thought my job was impossible. My empathy for all parents was clear, but my empathy for parenting in poverty was growing.

I convinced the clinic director to let me explore ways to enhance the program to better accommodate the needs of the women and their children. I thought we might create a drop-off infant/toddler playgroup to give babies a chance to be in an enriched child-development setting and mothers a chance to get a little time for themselves. I also thought that mothers could work in the playgroup next to trained child development specialists to get a little hands-on training that could accompany the home visiting and group sessions.

Before I could get the playgroup plans off the ground, the Federal Personal Responsibility and Work Opportunity Reconciliation Act of 1996 was signed into law, dramatically changing the social and political landscape of the neighborhood in which the clinic was based. The new act meant that parents of young children living in poverty would no longer be subsidized to stay home and care for their children. Rather than being subsidized to stay home and parent their young children, parents who had been dependent on welfare were suddenly shifting to paid work in temporary and low-wage jobs. In the absence of high-quality childcare, many young children lost significant parent contact, entered under-equipped childcare settings and received inconsistent care.

The government's new policies were aimed at getting single parents into the workforce in order to break generational cycles of welfare dependence, a laudable goal. But many mothers who had been on welfare had never worked before. Besides help finding jobs, they needed education and training. Some struggled to keep a job and/or welfare benefit eligibility.

The legislation required training and paying jobs for parents on public assistance—creating a huge gap between the supply of good childcare and the demand for it. There was some childcare funding provided (funding that has eroded significantly in the past decade), but no standards about the quality and consistency of care. Unfortunately, many policymakers and parents saw childcare as group babysitting—places for children to be safe while the parents are at work. It was seen only as a service that permits parents to enter the job market, not as an opportunity to promote child development.

Many mothers with infants and toddlers had no experience of their own mothers working. They did not know how to plan to best care for their children while they were at work or school, so their children bounced from care provider to care provider, from a paid program to family to friends and back to a paid program. Mothers had few choices and those choices they did have often resulted in inconsistent and unpredictable caregiving arrangements.

Winning employee of the month for a department in a national retail store, Darla beamed at her accomplishment. Having been in the "system" since age 6, when her mother died, Darla had worked hard to complete her high school degree and find a suitable job and childcare for her daughter, 1-year-old Alana.

As luck would have it, Darla's accomplishments became her downfall. During the busy retail season, her hours were changed to accommodate the store's busier night and weekend needs. Now working primarily evenings and weekends, Darla, a single mother, looked to various friends and neighbors to watch Alana while she worked. In response to losing her predictable routine and relationships with her childcare teachers, Alana became clingy. It was increasingly difficult for friends and neighbors to console her while her mother was at work. The alternative caregivers began to phone Darla while she was at work, asking her to leave early to pick up Alana.

Requests to her employer to reinstate her daytime hours failed. Darla was locked into the new schedule for at least 12 weeks, after which daytime hours were still not guaranteed.

Darla faced an impossible choice: her child or her job.

"Lots of people come here to study us and find out about problems like high infant-mortality rate, but they don't come back to help us. This program works with us to find solutions. Baby's Space has had a positive impact that goes beyond good childcare. Low-income communities often get bad services. Baby's Space gives us the best of everything, which helps lift the whole community up."

Parent at Little Earth

CREATING BABY'S SPACE

The neighborhood around the clinic where I was working had no high-quality childcare centers. Families struggling to take care of their families now had the enormous new challenge of managing parenting, childcare and work demands at the same time, all within a context of community violence, substance abuse and domestic violence. As a consequence, the vast majority of young children transitioned many times between childcare arrangements that were generally of poor quality and that lacked the individualized attention and responsiveness necessary for healthy development.

Instead of building playgroups, I—with help from the clinic director—formed a collaborative of nine community organizations and the University of Minnesota to address the needs of the families we were already serving who would now be adding consistent employment to their daily routines. Pooling resources, knowledge and expertise, we created a collaborative committed to finding ways to use current research and best practices to meet the new needs of families and young children. The collaborative came up with a commonsense solution to the childcare shortage as well as to persistent, generational poverty: provide extraordinary, research-based, culture-specific services to children and their families. Based on the group's recommendations, Baby's Space was formed in 1999.

Baby's Space was located in the Phillips neighborhood of south Minneapolis in a former Catholic elementary school that was redeveloped into an early learning center. This was part of the vision of the then-mayor and later Baby's Space board member,

Don Fraser. He envisioned neighborhood-based buildings in which early childhood programs would be co-located with other nonprofit organizations and agencies, allowing families with young children to easily access multiple services. This center was developed to respond to the cultures, values and needs of families in the Little Earth of United Tribes housing complex, which had approximately 800 residents, primarily American Indian. Nationally, a greater proportion of American Indians lived in poverty than any other group, at a rate that is nearly double the national average. In 1995 the annual income of the housing residents was $8,500 with 47 percent unemployment for the heads of households. Only three students living in the housing project graduated from high school (Hennepin County & Omniciye Program, 2009).

The negative impact on child development of poverty, unhealthy environments, violence, life stress and issues such as teenage pregnancy and poor educational attainment are cited in numerous studies. Research has shown that significant childhood adversity without the protection of a responsive, consistent and sensitive primary caregiver is responsible for differences in learning and behavior, and for higher risk for physical (cardiovascular and autoimmune diseases) and mental health disorders. Without the benefit of a protective relationship, children experience prolonged activation of their stress response systems, altering brain architecture for learning, memory, anxiety and fear.

Conversely, research that I was involved with demonstrated that secure relationships with parents moderated the impact of stress (Sroufe, Egeland, & Kreutzer, 1990). While preschool children reacted to stressful events, those with secure attachment relationships were able to regain typical development when stress passed. Children with a history of support and positive adaptations were protective factors against the negative effects of maternal life stress (Egeland & Kreutzer, 1990). And, we knew that quality of the relationship between mothers and their preschool children were more predictive of special education referrals than standardized test scores (Pianta, Erickson, Wagner, Kreutzer & Egeland, 1990). The quality of early parent-child relationships mattered, particularly in highly stressful environments.

The Native American community had been deeply traumatized. Its culture and history were dismissed by the majority culture for decades. For generations, the government sent Native American children to boarding schools, isolating them from their parents, culture and language. In Minnesota, the Native American community has had high rates of unemployment and the lowest rates of high school graduation (Wessle, 2009). Teen pregnancy has become an expectation, rather than an exception. For parents who have faced a history of marginalization, trauma, violence, poverty and alcoholism in the Native American community, a "good" relationship with their children may simply be the absence of harm. As one Native parent commented, "I like Baby's Space because nothing bad ever happens here."

The University of Minnesota, my employer, served as the fiscal agent for the childcare program. This was a high-risk venture for any of the other nonprofit organizations involved and the University, along with financial support from some of my friends, provided the umbrella we needed to get started. The community did not immediately welcome the University's presence. The services were needed, but University faculty had on numerous occasions come in with research proposals and promises. Our project was viewed with suspicion that we, too, would use the residents as test subjects and leave without improving the lives of those who participated. In fact, one of the first warnings I received was "don't take our kids' spit"—a concern created by a number of studies on the impact of environmental toxins that had preceded us.

In creating Baby's Space, we did not try to take things that had worked in full-day programs for older children and simply shrink them to preschool size; some early childhood programs look like miniature elementary classrooms, including the calculation of adult-to-child ratios. The elementary-school approach might help adults keep order and manage the day, but applying these same concepts to young children could have unintended negative affects. For example, in a program caring for babies and toddlers, the Minnesota maximum teacher-to-child ratios are 1:4 for babies and 1:7 for toddlers. After my experience of having three closely spaced young children, I could only imagine the challenges and responsibility of nurturing seven toddlers each day.

The Baby's Space program was built from the baby's point of view. We provided what a baby and family wanted and needed: loving relationships that are warm, sensitive, consistent and responsive, within a rich learning environment. These relationships grew in an enriched neighborhood-based setting that supported the whole family and featured best practices, proven models, holistic care—including parenting support and mental health services—and culturally relevant programming. In response to parent requests, we soon extended our services to include preschool and later opened a full-year kindergarten-through-third grade elementary school.

Parent engagement and support services were as vital as child services. Increasing the health and well-being of children by helping parents strengthen their families and build better relationships was the central goal. Through participation in education and support services, parents developed the understanding and capacity needed to nurture their children, support their academic achievements and ensure their future social and emotional success.

The baby's point of view was transformational.

Holding his dad's hand, 2-year-old Animkii is greeted by his teachers as he walks into his classroom. Animkii loves routines, so he immediately heads to his cubby to take off his coat. Leaving on the new baseball hat that Dad positioned sideways on Animkii's head, he goes straightaway to sit at one of the small a table on top of which is his favorite puzzle.

Dad signs the check in sheet on the counter and lets the teachers know that Animkii's grandmother will be picking him up in the afternoon. Dad fist pumps his son good-bye and reminds him to "be good." As dad exits the classroom, he nods his head with a quick lift of the chin towards the teachers.

> ### FROM THE BABY'S POINT OF VIEW
>
> For a 2-year-old, keeping on a carefully positioned baseball hat takes a lot of effort. But because his dad is so important to him, Animkii will do everything he can to keep the hat on as dad likes. Animkii moves carefully around the room to keep the hat in place. He yells at other children to make sure they don't bump it off of his head. When his teacher suggests that he put his hat in the cubby, he has big feelings and runs from the teacher. He insists on wearing the hat throughout the day, including while he napped on his cot. Similar to a blanket, teddy bear or other security item, the hat is his connection to his day while he is at childcare.

We worked side by side with families and customized support and education to respond to the strengths and needs of each child, parent and family. As a result, families' support networks, skills and resources are fortified, resulting in neighborhoods that are recreated in the best interest of children.

The hat provided a wonderful opportunity for the center director to work with dad and Animkii. From Animkii's perspective, the hat helped him feel connected with dad while he was at school and reminded him that his dad loves him. However, the director pointed out, toddlers are by nature messy and active and need freedom to explore. Keeping a hat on burdened a busy toddler with worry and apprehension—the opposite of what his dad wanted.

From the director's perspective, the hat seemed to say send a message, "My toddler is in the gang pipeline." She wondered, with dad, if that was what he wanted in the future for his son? Did he have a vision for Animkii that was different than gang membership? And how could he both protect and predict a successful future for his son?

A week later, the hat was no longer on Animkii's head—and dad stopped in the director's office wondering if she knew of resources for getting out of gang activity.

The initial outcomes for Baby's Space were terrific. Babies were developmentally on track and mothers were engaging in employment and education, delaying further pregnancies and understanding what it takes to successfully nurture their young children.

We felt that by providing consistency, predictability and security in long-range relationships with staff and the program we could create a secure base for both parents and children. Baby's Space was successful at engendering a strong and secure attachment relationship between children and their parents. But while secure infant-parent attachment relationships were necessary, we learned that they were not enough to guarantee success for young children growing up in neighborhoods of poverty and violence. By age 5, every child knew an adult who had been murdered, imprisoned or deported. These children were familiar with aspects of life that most adults believed should be no part of childhood.

Adults who have grown up in generational poverty, from whatever racial, ethnic or cultural background, have learned to survive, not necessarily to get ahead. We saw that parents often lacked a support network of friends and family. They had witnessed or personally experienced violence. They, or those they cared about, suffered from chemical abuse or mental health problems. Their poverty and other problems brought them into contact with the child protection system. We could see that adult behavior and perspectives were slow to change—no matter how consistent and accommodating the prevention and intervention services. Resources to support parenting—especially for those who haven't been parented themselves in secure, responsive ways and who live without economic benefit—must be consistent, adaptable, and expansive.

With the support of Baby's Space, children can learn at an early age that there are caring adults that can help them and their parents.

National Night Out is a yearly event where people get together with their neighbors to form connections that make a stronger neighborhood and help prevent crime. The city block on which Baby's Space sits had a street carnival for National Night Out, which included one of those giant inflatables for children to jump on.

Two of our Baby's Space children were waiting in line for the inflatable. As we would later learn, some teens got abusive and started hitting children who weren't theirs. The mother of the two Baby's Space children wisely pulled them from the line and went home.

The young mother did exactly the right thing, recognizing that she needed to protect her children. It was a huge step forward in her parenting. But the children didn't get to jump and play in the inflatable and they were upset.

The family could have come to the center angry the next day because the mother had done what Baby's Space wanted her to do, but not what her children wanted. Instead, they went to Debbie, the center director, with a plan. They asked if Baby's Space could have its own carnival. They said they knew Baby's Space would make sure the adults used their "school words."

Two weeks later, the school had its own carnival. Each child had a ticket for every station, so they knew ahead of time they would get to do everything at the carnival.

The child who led the charge for the carnival has become a self-appointed building monitor. A contractor working on the school building was talking on a cell phone one day and used the word "damn." The little boy went up to him, tugged on his pants leg and said, "Those aren't school words. Debbie will make you leave."

We continue on a journey that began in 1999 to keep vulnerable children from becoming casualties of poverty and trauma. Built on the premise that quality child development services offer a strategic and early intervention point for at-risk children, Baby's Space provides what a baby wants and needs: loving relationships that are warm, sensitive, consistent and responsive. These relationships grow in enriched environments featuring best practices, proven educational models, holistic care and culturally relevant programming—in the baby's neighborhood. Starting as a childcare center for infants, toddlers and their parents, we have expanded our childcare through third grade and now operate Tatanka Academy, a K-3 public contract alternative school in partnership with the Minneapolis Public Schools.

The Baby's Space full-spectrum model includes:

- High-quality care beginning at birth, provided by warm, committed and engaged teachers.
- Effective education extending through third grade.
- Parent education, family support and advocacy to develop successful children.
- Customized learning environments designed to promote developmental growth and strong relationships.
- Neighborhood-based location, increasing accessibility and transformational capacities.

Children at risk for developmental delays due to limits in the environment or parenting support receive the greatest benefit from integrated programs, which include both center-based early childhood education and parent services, such as home visiting. We do not replicate education models created for older children and simply shrink them down. Baby's Space's innovations in design, customer use and messaging of emotional health principles are transformational in early learning environments.

2

"Some of the most important learning we ever do happens
before we are born, while we are still in the womb."
Ann Murphy Paul

PRENATAL READINESS

When we think of preparing a child for success in school, most
of us don't realize just how early school readiness starts. But before
birth, the genetic blueprint that directs the development of the brain—
the foremost organ responsible for bodily functions, interpretation
of meaning, and rational thought—is in action. Through a universal
and fixed sequence of events, the location and function of brain
cells and the components for communication and coordination are
set. Knowing how the physical brain is formed prenatally provides
strong footing for our understanding of how construction of the
brain continues throughout childhood.

Unfortunately, there are experiences, exposures, and genetic
histories that alter brain construction and disrupt expected patterns of
prenatal brain development. As a result, some babies begin life and
learning with altered brain structure or neurochemical instructions that
deviate from typical development. That is, emotional readiness and
school success can be impaired by the absence of nutrients and vitamins,
presence of environmental toxins, and maternal health attributes that
occur before the baby is even born. Safeguarding prenatal development
needs to be at the foremost of our list of school-readiness strategies and
opportunities for supporting the health and well-being of all children.

"The fetus grows so rapidly during the first two
months that if the rate continued for the entire 9
month period, the baby would weigh 1.5 tons."
Alexander Tsiaras, MD

PRENATAL BRAIN DEVELOPMENT

The basic structure of the brain, like that of other organs and structures of the body, develops before the baby takes her first breath. The brain begins a period of rapid development after the baby is born that continues, as science is now revealing, throughout the person's lifespan—and this is unlike any other organ in the body. For example, the heart moves blood through the body in the same way on the day a baby is born that it will throughout that person's life; the function does not change. When you think of the multitude of functions the brain controls and how few of these capacities are present in a newborn, the true brilliance of the brain is revealed. It's essential to understand the basic architecture of the brain that should be present at birth and the potential threats to a sturdy foundation.

Neural Tube Development

During early pregnancy, the first major brain structure to form is the neural tube. Developing during the third week of gestation, the neural tube, which is the forerunner to the brain and spinal cord, is formed before many women know that they are pregnant. Because of the early and central nature of the neural tube, it's recommended that women take healthy measures before getting pregnant; adequate folic acid and vitamin B12, are particularly recommended (Calonge et al, 2009). Folic acid, one of the B vitamins, is important for promoting enzymes that help build the genetic materials, the blueprint for brain development. It's recommended that women of childbearing age consume folic acid every day to prevent brain defects and so to prevent neural tube defects, such as spina bifida, that may occur before most women have their first prenatal visit. These devastating birth defects impact one of every 1,000 pregnancies (Mathews, 2007).

> Shortly after returning home from a long-weekend trip to celebrate their anniversary, Destiny and her husband, Dan, discovered they were pregnant. The trip had been the first time they had taken a holiday together since the birth of their now 15-month-old son.
>
> The first signs of problems with the current pregnancy appeared at 12 weeks. At 18 weeks, the ultrasound confirmed that the baby had spina bifida. Destiny and Dan had not planned on becoming pregnant so soon, so Destiny, who took folic acid and multi-vitamins during her first pregnancy, had stopped after her first son was born. She resumed the folic acid and vitamins after discovering she was pregnant again at 8 weeks gestation—but it was already too late to prevent neural tube defects.
>
> Since nearly 50 percent of pregnancies are unplanned, the U.S. Preventive Services Task Force (2009) recommends that all women of childbearing age regularly take a 400 mg folic acid supplement for at least a year prior to pregnancy.

A recent study of 8,500 pregnant women in Norway found that folic acid also may help prevent autism (Suren et al, 2013). Women who took folic acid for at least one month before becoming pregnant and then continued to take folic acid for the first eight weeks of pregnancy were 40 percent less likely to have a child with autism. While the causal pathway has yet to be determined, neurobiological researchers believe that early brain growth may be a key factor in the pathobiology of autism (Courchesne et al, 2007).

Neuronal Genesis and Migration

During the first six months of prenatal development, the assembly of the brain's foundational structure is set. Following the creation of the brain stem by the sixth to seventh week of gestation, the next stage is the construction of more neurons, brain cells that will be responsible for the business of the brain—thinking, moving, feeling. This process, called neurogenesis, is in high gear for the first four months until it slows down at about 17 weeks gestation.

While initially created equally, what neurons do is determined by the location in the brain where they develop. A genetically controlled flow of chemicals moves neurons into different regions of the brain. Once neurons arrive at particular locations, the neurons receive the chemical information that directs the neurons to their functions and what type of brain cells each should become. For example, some neurons will efficiently interpret visual input, others will direct activities like breathing. Some neurons have more nuanced assignments, like processing emotions.

It is through these processes of migration and differentiations that neurons develop the capacities for specific activities. Interestingly, about 3 percent of neurons are misdirected and arrive at the wrong location. Researchers believe significant mislocations can result in permanent brain damage that is related to mental retardation, epilepsy, developmental delays and schizophrenia (McDonald, 2007).

Once a neuron reaches its specific location, it needs to communicate with other neurons with similar functions. To do this, the cell body develops surrounding branch-like structures, called dendrites. If you recall the familiar ad jingle "Can you hear me now?" or the childhood game of "telephone," you can think of dendrites as the receiver. After the dendrites sense signals from other neurons, the tail-like extension of the cell body, called the axon, is responsible for sending signals back to dendrites of neighboring neurons. Neurons seek other neurons that emit chemicals they like and repel neurons with unfamiliar chemicals. In this way, neurons reach out and communicate with their own affinity groups!

Directing brain efficiencies is the work of the later stage of gestation (and throughout the first twenty years of the child's life.) Before 7 months gestation, creating and connecting are the central activities. In fact, the brain overproduces the number of neurons needed and then begins the process of improving the speed and proficiency of communication (Rabinowicz et al, 2012).

At this stage, the brain can already demonstrate capacities for learning related activities (Joseph, 2000). From 20 to 27 weeks of gestation, the fetal brain will respond to loud sounds. By 28 weeks gestation, the fetus can recognize the mother's voice (DeCasper, Lecanuet, Busnel, Granier-DeFerre, & Maugeais, 1994). By 38 weeks, the fetus can recognize familiar from unfamiliar sounds. For example, researchers asked expectant mothers to read aloud a short children's rhyme each day between 33 and 37 weeks of their pregnancy. During the 38th week, the researchers found fetal heart rate differences when they played the familiar and unfamiliar rhymes (DeCasper et al, 1994).

The process of myelination (the formation of myelin, an insulating layer that protects nerves) begins around seven months and continues after the baby is born and throughout a good portion of childhood. Myelin protects the neuron and promotes speedier travel down the axon. We can see the evidence of myelination after birth when we watch a baby's arms go from flaying to a purposeful grasp. As the cognitive and motor neurons become more effective and speedier communicators, movement becomes smooth and intentional.

Because the process by which the brain develops is highly predictable and prescribed, a pregnant woman who takes her vitamins, eats nutritious foods, minimizes her stress and gets proper prenatal care dramatically improves the chances that her baby's brain structure will be healthy. It doesn't matter where in the world a pregnant woman lives; as long as she has adequate nutrition and a healthy environment, the sequence and structure ("hard wiring") of the brain, like other organs of the body, is expectably similar.

However, there are nuanced differences between brains. It is similar to what my plumber tells me when remodeling: The pipes aren't always exactly as drawn on the blueprints. Even brains of identical twins who share the same gene set have subtle differences in their brains' anatomy. The neural pathways that connect the back and front portions of the brain can be different in identical twins (Häberling, Badzakova-Trajkov, & Corballis, 2013). These dissimilarities in structure and function are most notable when one twin develops a significant brain disorder such as schizophrenia (Francks et al, 2007).

Much more common to all populations are the dissimilarities in neurological development that are revealed through handedness. Ninety percent of the population, no matter what region of the world, is right-handed. And the brain, by design is asymmetrical—that is that operations are centralized in the left or the right hemisphere. But for the 10 percent who are not right handed, the brain operates differently. In right-handed people, language abilities operate in the left hemisphere; in those who are left-handed or mixed-handed, language either occurs in both hemispheres or in the right hemisphere (Francks et al, 2007).

This may have valuable benefits—four of the last seven U.S. Presidents have been left-handed—but left-handedness or mix-handedness can present vulnerabilities. Using a large national study of young children that controlled for SES, parental attitudes and learning resources, researchers found that mixed-handed and, to a lesser degree, left-handed children performed significantly worse in nearly all measures of development than right-handed children, with the relative disadvantage being larger for boys than girls (Johnston, Nicholls, Shah, & Shields, 2009). In another study, dyslexia, an auditory processing disability that interferes with reading, was found to be associated with left-handedness (Scerri et al, 2011). Scientists believe that this type of variation, while increasing vulnerability, is part of human response to the adaptability of future generations.

*"We have 30,000 to 50,000 chemicals in our bodies
that our grandparents did not have."*
Penelope Jagessar Chaffer

PRENATAL RISKS TO DEVELOPMENT AND SCHOOL READINESS

Maternal Health

There are a variety of maternal, prenatal health concerns that can impact learning readiness and success of children. The most common maternal health concerns are those that may lead to premature births or and newborns with low birth weight. The CDC reports that one in every nine babies is born too soon, before 37 weeks gestation. Premature birth is particularly compromising for brain development. The brain of a baby born at 35 weeks weighs only two-thirds of what the brain would weigh if the baby were born at 39 weeks. The amount of growth, myelination and expansion in the brain between 35 and 39 weeks of gestation is considerable and is intended to happen while the fetus is growing and supported in the mother's womb. Once born, the requirements of the brain are essentially the same, even though the structure is underdeveloped.

A newborn that weighs less than 5 pounds, 6 ounces at birth is considered to have low birth weight. Seven out of 10 lower birth weight babies are premature, but full-term infants can also be at risk for low birth weight. Full-term newborns who weigh less than 90 percent of all babies are referred to "as small for gestational age." While some babies are physically healthy and small because their parents are small in stature, others are growth-restricted, meaning that expected growth slowed or stopped before birth. Most newborns are small because of growth problems during pregnancy that restricted nutrients and oxygen. Growth restriction is often related to maternal smoking, substance use, high blood pressure or malnutrition.

Newborns who are premature and/or underweight may have difficulties with hearing, vision and regulation of basic functions, such as sleep and body temperature. Those whose weight and height are significantly low have increased risk for lower cognitive abilities and poor school achievement (Paz et al, 1995). Prematurity and low birth weights often are associated with pregnancy with twins or other multiples, women living in poverty, racial disparities and teenage pregnancy (Isaacs, 2012; Reichman, 2005). A recent study revealed that premature birth and non-optimal fetal growth not only are associated with a variety of learning challenges, but also increase the risk for significant mental illnesses, including the need for hospitalization in adolescence and young adulthood (Nosarti et al, 2012).

Babies who are large for gestational age are also at risk for experiencing birthing complications and neurological and health challenges. Problems of large newborns are most often related to maternal weight and associated problems like diabetes. An estimated 60 percent of women who become pregnant are either overweight or obese. Forty percent of women who are normal weight when they become pregnant gain more during pregnancy than recommended by the Institute of Medicine (Josefson, Hoffmann & Metzger, 2013).

Maternal obesity is connected to increased risk of neural tube defect (Leddy, Power & Schulkin, 2008). The mechanism is still being studied, but there is evidence that obesity interferes with the transfer of nutrients to the embryo and fetus. Other researchers have found that, despite adequate maternal levels of Vitamin D at the time of birth, newborns of mothers with excessive weight gain had significantly lower levels of vitamin D (Josefson et al, 2013). These newborns are also two to three times more likely to be large for their gestational age and have more fat (adipose tissue) than babies of mothers who gain the recommended weight during pregnancy, and they are more likely to develop childhood and adult obesity and diabetes (Power, Cogswell & Schulkin, 2006).

Children who begin life with health challenges tend to have more difficulties with the skills necessary for school readiness and are at greater risk for poor school performance and cognitive difficulties, particularly in the areas of attention, emotional regulation and problem solving (Reichman, 2005).

Teratogens

There is increasing evidence that environmental changes can lead to long-term influences on the brain and behavior, interfering with school readiness (Boekelheide et al, 2012). A teratogen is a substance that can enter the intrauterine environment and cause birth defects. The most common teratogens are bacteria and viruses, drugs, alcohol, cigarette smoke and a variety of environmental toxins including mercury, lead, dioxin and radiation. Embryonic and fetal exposures change the chemistry that informs the neurons in the brain, disrupting the expected pattern of development. Teratogens also can interfere with the fetal repair system, rendering these alterations and developmental mistakes permanent (Schneider et al, 2008).

Alcohol

The most widespread and preventable brain damage is caused by prenatal exposure to alcohol and tobacco (March of Dimes, 2012). Within the first couple of weeks, the fertilized egg anchors to the mother and begins to share her blood supply. When alcohol enters the mother's bloodstream, it also surrounds the developing brain. If a mother smokes a cigarette or drinks a beer, so does the baby. Because the physical plant of the fetus is so much smaller than that of the mother, the period of inebriation lasts longer and is more intense. The concentration and impact of alcohol in the fetal bloodstream is much more extreme and the impact of binge drinking is a sudden flooding of the intrauterine environment, influencing all cellular and replication functions (Vaux & Chambers, 2010). At least 14 percent of women use alcohol or binge drink during pregnancy, making alcohol a leading cause of permanent brain dysfunction (Streissguth, Bookstein, Sampson, O'malley, & Young, 2004; Ethen et al, 2009).

Many women drink to numb or reduce the intensity of thoughts and feelings, an intensity that may be increased during pregnancy. Alcohol interferes with the communication of the manufacturing posts during the production of cells, particularly neurons. Alcohol in the fetal brain interferes with the production of neurons. Brains impacted by alcohol are smaller and abnormal in structure. There are fewer neurons to complete the anatomy. Alcohol also interferes with the migration or specialization of brain cells. For example, a brain cell intended for memory may go off-course or connect with neurons specializing in coordination. Alcohol mis-wires the brain permanently (Feldman et al, 2012).

The Centers for Disease Control (CDC) recommends that all women avoid alcohol during pregnancy. While a recent study reported in the British Journal of Obstetrics and Gynecology (Skogbero et al, 2012) reported no measurable impact on the executive functioning of 5-year-olds as a result of their mothers' low and moderate alcohol consumption, binge drinking (five drinks or more) showed a direct correlation with behavioral regulation and cognitive problems. A related study demonstrated that moderate drinking can significantly impact cognitive function, but the impact is moderated by the mother's and child's genetic make-up (Lewis et al, 2012).

> Being home full-time had not been the fulfilling adventure Jayne imagined it would be before leaving her successful career as a market analyst six years earlier. As she waited for the school bus to drop off her oldest child from first grade, she watched her 3-year-old play with a neighbor's daughter. To dull her dissatisfaction and boredom, she filled her coffee cup with wine each day. Sometimes it was only in the afternoon, but on certain days that were particularly difficult, she started pouring in the morning and didn't stop drinking until after the children were in bed. Now six months pregnant, she thought the red wine actually helped keep her calm. After all, she had read an article that stated that researchers found that a glass of wine was fine during pregnancy.

> But it wasn't fine. Justin was born at 36 weeks gestation. His head and eyes were smaller than expected. A heart

murmur was detected during a physical exam. In the nursery, the nurses noticed that he was extremely fussy and hard to soothe. He didn't seem to be able to latch on to the breast or to a nipple because his oral motor coordination was poor.

Jayne had been careful to hide her alcohol use. She bought wine in cases, telling the liquor store she was having a party. She disposed of the bottles at various playground dumpsters when she was at the park with her children. No one knew about the wine in the coffee cup, not even Jayne's husband. He knew she was unhappy, but he was unaware that she had been using alcohol regularly and sometimes stayed mildly intoxicated throughout the day.

Many of the developmental delays and learning difficulties are not recognized until the child begins school. Parents and teachers may notice that the child just "doesn't get" certain concepts or seems to gain and then lose skills. Problems with attention, following directions and cause-effect situations may be a struggle for a child with prenatal alcohol exposure. Foster and adoptive parents, particularly those with children from high-alcohol use countries like Russia, may be devastated to learn of their children's permanent brain dysfunctions.

The impact of fetal alcohol is enormous and costly for the child, family, school system and society. The medical and special education expenditures for these children are nine times higher than for non-impacted children and nearly twice as high than for children with autism spectrum disorder or sickle cell anemia (Mvundura, Amendah, Sprinz, Kavanagh, & Grosse, 2009). A study of school-age children estimated that fetal alcohol effects impact seven out of every 1,000 children (May, et al, 2009). According to the

CDC (2010), there is no period in prenatal development or amount of alcohol that is safe for the unborn child.

Smoking

Maternal smoking rates during pregnancy are the highest for teenagers and young adults. In 2005, 17 percent of 15- to 19-year-old women and 19 percent of women ages 20 to 24 smoked during pregnancy (CDC, 2007). The rates are even higher for those who live below the poverty line. Smoking during pregnancy exposes the fetus to nicotine, tar and carbon monoxide; decreases oxygen flow; and slows fetal growth. Smoking creates an increased likelihood that a baby will be born prematurely, have low birth weight and/or be underweight for gestational age—all risk factors for future learning problems. These risk factors can be greatly reduced when a woman does not smoke during pregnancy. The likelihood of a child being ready for school if his mother smoked during pregnancy is 10 percent lower than it is for a child whose mother did not smoke (Issacs, 2012).

Illicit Drugs

Many of us remember the news images of poor, black, addicted women that led to prejudiced legislative responses such as criminal charges against mothers who delivered babies with crack in their system and that made the term "crack baby" a familiar household phrase. Perhaps more than with any other illicit drug, public opinion seems to have led science, rather than the other way around, when it comes to issues around cocaine and crack—including prenatal exposure. This contrasts with a good portion of research that shows that cocaine and its derivatives do not have the long-term, irreversible negative effects that once were suspected. Heightened concerns about crack cocaine stemmed from ideas about who was using the drug as much as (or maybe even more than) what was happening as a result of that use. Pregnant women who use alcohol and nicotine have not suffered from widespread condemnation the same way crack and cocaine users have, yet the long-term damaging prenatal effects of alcohol and nicotine have been more consistently documented (Lester & Twomey, 2008).

The literature on the effects of specific illicit drug use during pregnancy is limited. Because most women who use illicit drugs are poly-users—that is, they also engage in smoking and drinking alcohol and live under stressful life conditions—it is difficult to isolate and attribute outcomes to one specific illicit substance. Savvy researchers have been incorporating poly-use into the research design, allowing researchers to compare groups of pregnant women who used a particular illicit drug along with alcohol with those who used an illicit drug but did not use alcohol and those who used neither drugs nor alcohol (Sowell et al, 2010).

Although marijuana is the most frequently used illicit drug among pregnant women, little research has been done on its effects on the developing fetus. The body of literature on prenatal marijuana exposure is limited and inconsistent, with some studies citing long-term deficits in school achievement aggressive behavior and fetal growth reduction (Day, Leech & Goldschmidt, 2011).

Methamphetamine is unique in its ability to impact the child both prenatally, through maternal use, and postnatally through environmental exposure. Particularly if a baby is in a home where meth is cooked, the baby's exposure may continue as she inhales, swallows toxic substances or absorbs meth through the skin while sleeping on contaminated bedding. Meth users often go days without sleeping or eating, further disrupting the intrauterine environment.

Like most of the other high school students on a summer Friday night, Laura drank beer and took shots of whiskey outside of the Dairy Queen on Main Street. Students gathered around the parked cars, talking and horsing around. There wasn't much else to do on a sweltering evening in this northern resort community. When someone suggested that the group go skinny-dipping in a local lake, Laura turned to her cousin and pleaded, "Let's go home. I don't want anyone to see me in a bathing suit, let alone naked."

Laura's cousin had recently been losing weight and was eager to show off her new figure. "Here, take this," said the cousin as she handed Laura the tablet form of meth. "It's how I'm losing weight! Plus, it will put you in a really good mood."

By the end of the summer, 15 year-old Laura, was 10 pounds lighter, regularly using meth and pregnant. Convinced that she couldn't get pregnant, Laura ignored the early signs of pregnancy. By the end of the first semester, she was hiding a small belly bump with the high school uniform of sweatshirt and pants. The meth helped her control her eating, which limited weight gain. Laura could not tell her cousin about the pregnancy for fear that the cousin would tell Laura's father and mother, who would be devastated to discover that their honor roll daughter was having sex.

The unborn baby pulled most of the nutrients Laura was consuming so that her hair began to fall out and her teeth to develop cavities. Her parents worried that staying up all night and significant periods of moodiness were something more than the teenage angst of finals and friends.

Prenatal methamphetamine exposure is associated with fetal growth restriction and structural abnormalities in the developing fetus' brain (Nguyen et al, 2010, Lu et al, 2009). Infants exposed to meth are found to experience extreme fussiness, sensitivities to stimulation and neurological impairments, and often are difficult to comfort. These behaviors make parenting a baby with prenatal meth exposure more difficult (Twomey et al, 2013).

Because of the relative recent rise of meth use in pregnant

women, longitudinal studies are just beginning. Researchers examining a national sample of children who were prenatally exposed to meth have found behavioral differences at age 3 and age 5 (LaGasse et al, 2012, Twomey et al, 2013). Early expressions of anxiety/depression and emotional reactivity were detected at age 3 and continuing at age 5. In addition, at age 5, children prenatally exposed to meth were more aggressive and had symptoms consistent with Attention Deficit Hyperactive Disorder (ADHD).

Using brain scans, researchers have discovered that the use of methamphetamine during pregnancy may produce greater changes to brain structure than alcohol. Meth seems to have an added impact on specific areas of brain architecture: the caudate nucleus, responsible for learning and memory, and the cingulated cortex, which is involved in the processing of emotions and conflict resolution. Two studies have compared prenatal alcohol exposure to prenatal alcohol and methamphetamine exposure, and found that the effects of methamphetamine and alcohol combined are more damaging than the effects of alcohol alone (Lu et al, 2009, Sowell et al, 2010).

Environmental toxins

Some of the strongest environmental teratogens are ones a woman has little control over: the air she breathes, the neighborhoods she walks through every day, the way she is treated in her community and society. For pregnant women in poverty, living in old houses with lead-based paint and exposures to toxins are at a disproportionately high rate. A pregnant woman can do a number of things to minimize or prevent toxic exposures, but these exposures, which may have mild or moderate impact on the development of the brain, are invisible to most and easily dismissed as inconsequential (Grason & Misra, 2009). Particularly for women living in poverty, removing shoes upon entering the house to reduce lead exposure or buying local apples that have not been sprayed with DDT are luxuries they may not be able to afford.

The center that I founded is located across from a housing development that is six blocks from an area designated in 2007 as a national superfund site for soil contamination. According to the EPA's website, for years the wind blew the arsenic-contaminated soil throughout several neighborhoods of south Minneapolis. The pollution was discovered in 2004 on 1,480 acres of land that was the home, from 1938 to 1963, of a company that produced arsenic-based pesticides. The site's final cleanup phase was completed in 2011 (Environmental Protection Agency [EPA], 2012). The EPA removed 50,000 tons of contaminated soil from this densely populated residential area.

It is alarming to look at the effects of arsenic on prenatal development (Singh et al, 2012). Prenatal exposure to arsenic increases the risk for respiratory diseases like asthma, diabetes, rheumatoid arthritis and cardiovascular disease (Boekelheide et al, 2012). A high arsenic level in pregnant women quintuples the likelihood of low-birth weight babies and death before age 1 (Rahman et al, 2010). Ongoing exposure to arsenic is related to lower IQ, growth and learning.

When constructing a new recreation center at the end of the block from our school, the city again encountered the contaminated lead. The 50-foot-high pile of dirt resulting from the hole created for the building's footings was contaminated with arsenic, lead and asbestos. Unable to easily dispose of the soil, the pile was causally covered with plastic tarps and left for months while the city figured out where to dump the toxic soil (Liu, McDermott, Lawson & Aelion, 2010). The pile was not fenced off, warning signs were not posted and the plastic tarps began wearing. Wind blew the loose soil. The neighborhood wading pool was closed but not the playground next to it or the housing development nearby. Contaminants in the soil enter the body when the dirt gets on hands and those hands touch mouths.

A national survey of obstetricians found that most physicians routinely concentrate on prenatal issues related to obesity, hypertension, use of alcohol and tobacco, but frequently don't warn patients about hazards in the environment, food and products (Grason & Misra, 2009). The study found that many doctors didn't feel confident in their knowledge of the topics and did not want to cause undo anxiety for expectant mothers and fathers. For example: 300,000 or one out of 14 babies are born with mercury levels that are known to reduce IQ and impact brain development. Yet, only 40 percent of obstetricians discuss avoiding mercury-contaminated food, including tuna and swordfish.

"Lifestyle decisions you make today can still effect future generations."
Courtney Griffins, PhD

EPIGENETICS

Each person's genetic code or DNA is similar to a set of blueprints, and each cell in that person's body has the exact same blueprints. These blueprints determine the color of the iris, hair and skin, as well as the shape of the nose, the length of the fingers and the appearance of dimples. Understanding the genetic code has been an ongoing scientific pursuit. Most of us can remember the principles of inherited traits and the studies of Mendel who cross-bread pea plants from high school biology—and we remember that it took many, many generations for the giraffe to develop a neck that can reach into trees for food without making it too difficult to walk.

Intended to gather and store information about the function of human genes, the human genome project began in 1990 with the hope of finding a straightforward cause-and-effect relationship between gene structure and disease development (U.S. Department of Energy Genome Programs, 2012). Instead, what the scientists found was that disease-related genes were present, in many cases, without disease. That is, a person can be walking around with a gene sequence known to produce a disease but never experience the symptoms.

There is now a growing body of evidence that a variety of experiences or environmental stimuli can produce changes in the function of the DNA sequence. That is, within the cell, the genetic code is the same but, through chemical processes that operate at the cellular level, instructions are given about when and which parts of the cell's DNA sequence to activate. Think about a conference hall that has multiple switches with dimmer adjustments for the hall's lighting. All of the individual lights are present at all times, but the switches control which sequence of lights are on and off and how brightly they shine.

Researchers have come to understand that some chemical interactions can change the function of genes. They have termed these phenomena the epigenome: operations above or on the genetic code. A relatively new field of study has emerged, epigenetics, which is revealing how genes are engaged in an ongoing interaction to create health or disease through a cellular chemical process. Scientists are gathering evidence that environment and genetics are inextricably linked in such a way that neither is more important than the other. This is particularly relevant to our work with young children and learning because the epigenetic process is most active during pregnancy, when the timing, composition and sequence of embryonic and fetal development are determined by a set of highly structured, genetically controlled chemical events.

The Agouti gene is responsible for hair color and patterns in mammals, including dogs, cats and horses. In mice, chemical interactions can turn on the Agouti gene, resulting in a yellow-coated mouse with a high incidence of obesity and related diabetes and cancer, or turn off the Agouti gene, resulting in a thin, brown-haired mouse with a low incidence of disease (Wolff, Kodell, Moore, & Cooney, 1998). Genetically identical mice can look dramatically different and encounter different diseases depending on whether the switch for this gene is in the "on" or "off" position. Using the conference hall light analogy, if all the lights are on, obesity and disease result.

Scientists discovered that when pregnant Agouti mice are exposed to high levels of a chemical, bisphenol-A or BPA, commonly found in beverage and food containers, the number of yellow, obese offspring increased dramatically (Chaddha, 2007). When chemically exposed pregnant mice were fed a diet rich in soy, known to counterbalance the chemical processes of BPA, more of the offspring were slender and brown; in these offspring, the gene activity was turned "off."

In a study of the impact of maternal exposure to pesticides on cognitive development of children, researchers found that the impact depended on the mother's genetic makeup. One third of the urban mothers in the study had a genetic coding that produced a weaker enzyme and resulted in greater cognitive impairments in their children (Engel et al, 2011).

Generational Impact

It now appears the epigenetic changes can impact successive generations.

> A group of researchers exposed adult lab rats to a toxin and, as expected, the rats developed toxic-related diseases not common in typical lab rat colonies. What was most interesting about this study was not the illnesses in the exposed rats, but the persistence of these illness in their offspring and their offspring's offspring. From an epigenetic perspective, it appeared that the toxin turned on a disease process that, once activated, was passed along from generation to generation.
>
> When the researchers combined the third generation of rats who were likely to develop toxic-related diseases with rats from a typical lab rat colony, the female rats from the typical colony would not mate with the males from the toxic line. Interestingly, the researchers found that the healthy colony male rats would mate with females from both colonies (Crews et al, 2007).

In another study using rats, first-generation offspring of a healthy colony were subjected to a restricted and poor quality diet. Their offspring and their grand-offspring received adequate nutrition, but the grand-offspring had poor physical growth and poor performance in maze learning when compared with pups from grandparents who received proper nutrition throughout (Jablonca & Lamb, 1995).

Depression and Anxiety

There is a growing body of evidence that it's not only external events and exposures that result in epigenetic changes. Psychological experiences of pregnant mothers—depression, anxiety and high levels of life stress—also influence prenatal development of children and set the stage for behavioral, health and learning differences in their children (Weinberg & Tronick, 1998; Tronick, 2012). Traditionally, we have referred to prepartum and postpartum depression as something unique to pregnancy and early parenting. Our current thinking is that, for many women, these symptoms are reoccurrences of symptoms they experienced during other periods of their lives, rather than something unique to pregnancy.

A recent study by the Minnesota Children's Defense Fund (2011) revealed that at least 10 percent of women (and their unborn children) experience depression. The rates are higher for women who have limited social support and significant financial limitations, and for teens and women from minority cultures. A large-scale study by Northwestern University reported that 14 percent of the women screened positive for depression (Wisner et al, 2013).

Women who were diagnosed with depression during pregnancy had an increased incidence of premature labor and delivering a baby with low birth weight or fetal growth restriction, compared with those who were not depressed (Diego et al, 2009). When a pregnant woman has overwhelming feelings of sadness, hopelessness or worry, the chemical make-up of the fetal environment is altered.

Studies indicate that, for children born to these mothers, the emotional center of the brain develops differently than that of infants whose mothers did not experience depression (Dawson et al, 1999; Oberlander et al, 2008). Research strongly suggests that babies whose mothers are depressed demonstrate reduced activity in the area of the brain that mediates social behaviors and positive expression (Dawson et al, 1999). Following birth, newborns of depressed mothers are fussier and more irritable and appear to have less mature regulatory systems (Field, Diego & Hernadez-Reif, 2006). They may have more difficulty calming themselves and require more, not less, adult support to regulate sleep, eating and engaging with others. Babies of mothers with depression are more likely to have chaotic sleep patterns in the first year of life than babies born to non-depressed moms, and to have difficulty establishing typical circadian rhythms.

Behavior problems in children during toddler, preschool and elementary years are associated with maternal depression in a child's first year of life (Carter, Garrity-Rokous, Chazan-Cohen, Little & Briggs-Gowen, 2001). For these children, the areas controlling the emotional center of the brain develops differently than those of infants whose mothers are not experiencing depression (Dawson, et al, 2003; Oberlander et al, 2010). Specifically, the area of the brain specialized for negative emotion shows more activity while the area correlating to positive emotion shows less activity.

While it is common for a woman to be nervous about pregnancy, the health of her unborn baby and the ensuing life transitions, overwhelming worry, intrusive thoughts, an inability to relax or sleep and panic attacks may be signs of an anxiety disorder. Prenatal anxiety has been found to increase behavioral problems at age four (O'Conner, Heron, Glover & Alspace Study Team, 2002). The environmental alterations of the intrauterine environment attributable to mood and stress seem to have had structural impact on the developing baby that resulted in lasting changes in how the stress-response system functions (Oberlander et al, 2008).

Changes in fetal physiology have also been found with anxiety in pregnant women. Women who experience anxiety during pregnancy are found to have a faster resting heart rate than those without anxiety. Under resting conditions, however, there is no difference in fetal heart rate for mothers experiencing anxiety. Yet, under mildly stressful situations, fetal heart rates increase in anxious mothers but not for fetuses of non-anxious pregnant women. Prenatal anxiety is also associated with an increased risk of asthma at age 7 (Cookson, Granell, Joinson, Ben-Shlomo & Henderson, 2009). Elementary-age children whose mothers experienced high levels of anxiety related to their pregnancies performed less well on tests of visual working memory, and girls showed more difficulty with inhibition (Buss, Davis, Hobel, & Sandman, 2011).

Life Stress

Stress may be the strongest emotion-related risk to a developing baby. In response to a stressful situation, the brain triggers chemical reactions to help the body react. Chronic maternal stress during pregnancy can compromise the body's attempt to balance, thereby elevating placental hormones that can result in slowed fetal growth, preterm labor and delivery and reduced birth weight (Talge, Neal & Glover, 2007). Chronic stress can lead to changes in an unborn baby's heart rate and cortisol, the chemical produced to respond to immediate threat or danger. In pregnant women, cortisol binds to receptors in the placenta, which causes a reaction that can induce premature labor and reduce the blood flow to the growing baby.

Using animal studies, researchers have been able to document the epigenetic impact of chronic stress. By consistently stimulating pregnant rhesus monkeys with stress hormones for a period of two weeks, researchers found that the offspring of these mothers had impaired motor coordination, poor muscle tonicity and shorter attention spans, and were more irritable and difficult to console than the offspring of non-stressed mothers.

When the World Trade Center collapsed in 2001, many women near the epicenter of the disaster were pregnant. Researchers who followed those women found that the psychological trauma, as measured by post-traumatic stress symptomatology (PTSD), resulted in a decrease in head circumference of their newborns, which may in turn be related to later neurocognitive developmental problems (Engel, Berkowitz, Wolff & Yehuda, 2005). In a prospective study, Danish researchers were able to connect stress experienced during pregnancy with a number of negative child health outcomes, including behavioral disorders during infancy and toddlerhood and increased risk of infections, respiratory illnesses and congenital malformations (Tegthoff, Greene, Olsen, Schaffner & Meinlschmidt, 2011). Toddlers whose mothers experienced high levels of stress, particularly early in the pregnancy, demonstrated lower general intellectual and language abilities (Laplante et al, 2004). Pregnant women with PTSD passed on a vulnerability to their children while still in utero.

> Following emergency family leave for her mother's funeral, Nora and her husband are surprised to discover that they are pregnant. With two months left in her second deployment to Afghanistan, Nora was anxious to return home for the remainder of her pregnancy.
>
> Once home however, she was surprised by her unyielding worries about her unborn child. Nora was concerned about the pregnancy—and particularly afraid that the things she saw and did during her deployment had impacted her motherly instincts. She was fraught with guilt and anxiety.
>
> Additionally, she and her husband were struggling to reconnect. They knew that many of their fellow service members struggled during the first few months of reunification, but for Nora, the frequent arguments about everything from what to watch on television to who washed the dinner dishes were overwhelming. Below the surface was tension about how to prepare for the birth of their baby. Before Nora's first deployment, the couple had experienced three miscarriages. Nora's choice to enlist for active duty was in part to separate from the pain of those failed pregnancies.

While our reaction is to reassure Nora that her baby and her ability to mother will not be impaired by her deployment, science is revealing that chronic stress and untreated depression and anxiety can lead to changes in the intrauterine environment with epigenetic effects. Chronic stress and depression during pregnancy are linked with preterm delivery, and depression and anxiety increase the likelihood of lower birth weight—birth outcomes related to poorer health and academic progress for children. Researchers found that when women who were diagnosed with depression during pregnancy were compared with pregnant women who were not depressed, the depressed pregnant women had a 13 percent greater incidence of premature labor and a 15 percent greater incidence of a baby with low birth weight (Grote, et al, 2010).

Chronic stress, untreated depression and anxiety can lead to persistent changes in an unborn baby's heart rate and cortisol. In a study of moderation of the effects of stress, researchers found that in a sample of pregnant women from Los Angeles County, 21.6 percent of African American women reported the chronic stress, as well as experiencing more stressful life events, than other ethnic groups (Ghosh, Wilhelm, Dunkel-Schetter, Lombardi & Ritz, 2010).

Fathers and Epigenetics

Often, generational health outcome data focuses on the well-being of mothers. In an animal study in which male adult mice were subjected to extreme and repetitive attacks by a larger, dominant mouse, the male mice developed a number of pathological behaviors that would be similar to depression, post-traumatic stress disorder and anxiety (Dietz et al, 2011). When healthy female mice were impregnated with sperm from these compromised male mice, the offspring were avoidant of other mice and over-reactive to social stress, and demonstrated signs of depression and anxiety.

The epigenetic impact of the health and experiences of fathers is limited, but early indications are that the experience of males may be equally as influential in switching genetic coding on and off.

Researchers speculated that there would be trans-generational effects from male smoking before puberty—another period of development when epigenetic effects are particularly powerful—on the growth patterns of the men's offspring (Pembrey et al, 2006). Studying who began smoking as early as age 10 demonstrated that the sons of men who began smoking before puberty and who continued to smoke during the time they conceived were at greater risk for obesity and other health-related problems into adulthood. These epigenetic effects were complicated and based both on a sensitive period (pre-puberty smoking) and sex specific toxicity (only sons). The impact had life-long health consequences for the offspring.

Trans-generational epigenetic inheritance of disease and impairments in development are revealed in the epigenetic research. One of the first and most interesting epigenetic human studies shows generational differences in response to environmental events. Using historical records, agricultural and life expectancy data were collected from the isolated Swedish village of Overkalix in the county of Norrbotton, which was completely cut off from the mainland until the twentieth century. Using records beginning in 1779, researchers were able to follow health outcomes of successive generations (Kaati, Bygren & Edvinsson, 2002).

Drawing a random sample of individuals whose ancestors experienced environmental fluctuations, the scientists were able to trace outcomes for 99 individuals born in 1905. According to exceptionally accurate and extensive historical documents maintained by the Swedish government, the citizens of Overkalix experienced extreme starvation during the time of bad harvests, and gorged to the point of gluttony when crops were in abundance. Researchers discovered several health outcomes related to the experiences of starvation and gluttony.

When boys right before puberty, between the ages of 9 and 12, experienced poor nutritional conditions and scarcity of food, they had lower than expected rates of heart disease as adults. When the boys enjoyed the rare overabundant winter gluttony, they were unknowingly impacting the health history of their grandsons, who had higher rates of diabetes. On average, sons and grandsons of men who had experienced a period of gluttony just before puberty died six years sooner than those whose ancestors did not experience gluttony. The study concluded that nutrition had a generational impact on males, which changed the risk for cardiovascular disease and diabetes (Kaati et al, 2002).

This data motivates us to rethink our consideration of the impact of historic environmental events, particularly for children from specific at-risk populations. It may not be only the current conditions of the child's experience, but also the ancestral experiences of extreme deprivation, trauma, slavery, forced labor or chemical exposures that have changed the expressions of the genetic coding, impacting health, learning and behavior. Some environmental conditions are beneficial and may increase resistance or decrease vulnerability, depending on the meaning of the event to the individual and the translation of the event genetically from generation to generation.

"Preconception and prenatal care can help prevent complications and inform women about important steps they can take to protect their infant and ensure a healthy pregnancy."

National Institutes of Health

PROMOTION OF HEALTHY PRENATAL DEVELOPMENT

While our assumption is that all babies are born ready to learn, some may have hidden and unexpected weaknesses in their foundations for learning and emotional health. Early in pregnancy, the health of the mother and her nutrition, use of medication and behaviors impact the production and distribution of brain cells. The data reveals that not all babies start with the same sturdy and ready-to-learn brain structure. Since the development of more complex skills is dependent on having the prescribed physical structure in place, these children may face vulnerabilities before they speak their first words. School readiness is not only an issue of getting 5-year-olds ready to read, but also making sure that the 5-month-old fetus has adequate nutrition and is maturing within a toxin-free environment.

Let's revisit maternal risk related to potential compromises for the baby's chances for learning and emotional success:

- 60 percent of women are obese or overweight during pregnancy and 40 percent of typical weight women gain more than they should while pregnant.
- 14 percent of women use alcohol or binge drink during pregnancy.
- 13 percent of pregnant women smoke; 19 percent of 20- to 24-year-old pregnant women smoke.
- 10 percent of pregnant women experience untreated depression and anxiety.
- 8 percent of women experience post traumatic stress disorder during pregnancy.
- 8 percent of pregnant women are victims of intimate partner violence.
- 7 percent of pregnant women are less than 19 years old.

- 7 percent of women do not seek prenatal care until the third trimester (USHSS, 2011)
- 1,312 U.S. sites are on the EPA's National Priorities List for toxic cleanup.
- 25 percent of pregnant women and children live in homes with deteriorating lead-based paint and are at risk for lead exposure (American Academy of Pediatrics, 2005).
- 7 percent of pregnant women are exposed to levels of methylmercury that exceed the federal guidelines.

These percentages are based on the U.S. population as a whole. Many of the negative outcomes double for specific populations when income, age and/or minority status are included.

These are the numbers after the widely successful public health campaigns and the efforts of thousands of local and national programs. There has been a reduction in teenage pregnancies, the number of pregnant women who do not receive adequate prenatal care and preterm deliveries. But, borrowing from a new campaign slogan designed to reduce the number of children who smoke, there is "still a problem."

Here is what we know about the observable risks for newborns (March of Dimes, 2012; CDC 2008):

- 12 percent of births in the United States are preterm.
- 10 percent of newborns will be left-handed.
- 10 percent of full-term newborns are large for gestational age.
- 3 percent of full-term newborns have experienced intrauterine growth problems and are significantly under-weight.
- 3 percent of babies are born with birth defects.
- 1.1 percent of babies born today will be diagnosed with autism, based on current rates.

Most individual women receive guidance before and during pregnancy through their primary health care provider and obstetrician. There are a number of best practices that involve primary medical care for women before and during pregnancy. It is recommended (Moos, 2002) that physicians pay particular attention to women who have had unplanned pregnancies, spontaneous abortions or repeat pregnancies within 12 months, or who have experienced fetal or newborn deaths. For these women, beyond supplying basic medical care, health care providers are encouraged to develop personal pre-pregnancy health plans, implement preventative and health improvement strategies, mobilize healthy patient support systems, facilitate transportation and other issues related to accessing medical services and provide mental heath support.

While having a well-woman healthcare "home" and proper prenatal health care are unquestionably essential, this limits the responsibility of ensuring healthy pregnancies and brain development to the provider and the pregnant woman. A recent survey of obstetricians found that, while there are concerns over the impact of excessive weight gain on their patients, many are unsure how to address the issues without offending, stigmatizing or discouraging the women (Stotland et al, 2010; Yonkers et al, 2009). Researchers also found that only 40 percent of physicians discuss avoiding mercury in fish, the deleterious effects of cleaning products or other environmental or job-related health risks. In many ways, even with appropriate care, these are not issues that a physician can fix in an office visit. We need to rethink what an individual woman who is pregnant, living in the housing project next door to the superfund toxic cleanup site, with limited access to a food store that carries affordable fruits and vegetables, needs to do to have a healthy baby.

The good news is that there are many, many things that we as communities and families can do to safeguard our youngest and most vulnerable future citizens, if we recognize the significance of healthy pregnancies and the impact of toxins, stress, mental health and maternal wellness on neurodevelopment and later school success. By empowering women, families and communities, we can capitalize on the capacities of individuals, neighborhoods and cultures to safeguard maternal and child well-being. For example, a recent study found that a supportive spouse moderates the effects of chronic stress on the risk of preterm delivery (Goush et al, 2009). Healthy eating habits during pregnancy, combined with an active lifestyle, help prevent long-term risk of obesity for both the mother and her child. With the inclusion of evidenced-based research, local community efforts to increase the preconception health of women, improve maternal nutrition, reduce teenage pregnancy and facilitate early health management can go a long way in protecting the brain development of young children.

Preconception Health Care

Optimally, the health of all women is important, regardless of pregnancy intentions. For most women, our own well-being takes a back seat to the needs of those around us. It is difficult to prioritize our own health without feeling selfish that we are taking time and resources away from more important responsibilities. Perhaps by focusing on the well-being of children, women can prioritize their own well-being in the context that healthy moms—before, during and after pregnancy—have healthier children.

Well-defined health indicators for the period prior to pregnancy, considered preconception health, are defined by Healthy People 2020 (HHS, 2011):

- One month before pregnancy, taking multivitamins/folic acid.
- Not smoking three months before pregnancy.
- Not drinking alcohol for three months prior to pregnancy.
- Healthy weight.

A pillar of preconception healthcare is the creation of a reproductive life plan, which allows women and their partners to think about goals for having or not having children. With plans in place, women can more easily decide how and when to change behaviors, for example drinking alcohol. Knowing that life can be unpredictable, women may decide to take vitamin and folic acid supplements and make lifestyle changes, including exercise, to help ensure the health and well-being of their future pregnancies and children (Ruchat & Mottola, 2012).

For some women, some of the lifestyle changes can feel monumental. Remember, 60 percent of women at the time of pregnancy are distinctly overweight. For long-term success, women need to develop skills, self-awareness and the motivation to make the necessary changes for their own health and well-being and that of their future children.

At Baby's Space, we are using Personal Empowerment training, developed by Twin Cities RISE!, an organization founded by Steve Rothschild, a former General Mills executive vice president and an Ashoka Fellow, to assist low-income adults get living-wage jobs. Our Personal Empowerment groups focus on personal skill-building to improve self-awareness, emotional regulation and self-esteem, so women can make the internal changes necessary to transform their health. The empowerment groups allow women to prioritize their own healthcare by completing their reproductive plan and making the necessary changes in behaviors that will lead to healthier lifestyles, pregnancies and babies.

The commitment to prioritizing health must come from within the person, but a community of support that reflects this priority is essential. Often, in the afternoon at work or in a staff meeting, someone is offering cookies or other tempting sweets. Rejecting them can be seen as being dismissive of kindness, culturally offensive or snobbish. No one comes around with a plate of vegetables, almonds and hummus saying, "I care about you."

Finding or creating social systems that prioritize health and support healthier lifestyles is extraordinarily important for most people to make lifestyle/health changes. This is a place where family, peer groups and culture can be tremendously helpful or divisive. The work of Rick Warren and the Daniel Plan, which started as a health plan addressing health and fitness at a church and then spread into a multi-faith movement, is a remarkable example of focusing individuals' needs for both internal motivation and external support.

"I am pregnant for the first time and am due soon. Do women feel depressed prior to pregnancy and lose their own identity? I know I'm going to be a mom—but I'm not sure I want to be. At the same time, I'm excited about being a mom. It's confusing."

Pregnancy and Birth Support

Pregnancy and childbirth offer subtle and fleeting windows of opportunity to help parents develop a special connection with their babies. The way a mother thinks about her unborn child becomes linked with her view for the world in general. The more a mother can think about her unborn child and articulate what the future will be like, how the child will change her life and what the impact of the birth will be, the more her commitment to her baby increases.

Community-based programs that provide groups or individual pregnancy education and support services can promote healthy, educated, realistic attitudes and expectations about pregnancy, childbirth and parenting in the form of prenatal support. Individual support, particularly when the supporter is from the same community as the mother, can be a powerful way to help the pregnant woman imagine what it will be like to give birth and to be a mother. Doulas promote healthier birth outcomes by helping women develop realistic attitudes and expectations about pregnancy, childbirth and parenting, and by celebrating the parent-child relationship. Baby's Space doulas offer childbirth education, attend medical appointments, create a birth plan with the family and provide hands-on emotional and physical support throughout labor and delivery.

At age 19, Natalie was single, homeless and pregnant. Her uncle let her sleep on his couch in his apartment in an urban low-income housing development. When she went into labor, her uncle walked her to the corner to meet the cab. She went to the hospital, labored and delivered her daughter with no family or friends to support her. No one came to visit her. She was glad that the nurses were "really nice."

Two years later, Natalie was expecting her second baby. The Baby's Space family facilitator who was trained as a doula had been working with Natalie since her first child was enrolled in the childcare center. Natalie made a warm connection with the facilitator and enjoyed play dates at childcare, as well as regular home visits. The facilitator supported Natalie's regular medical visits and, with the father of the unborn baby, the family facilitator helped create a birth plan and discussed resources for the baby. As her pregnancy neared its end, Natalie had almost daily contact with the facilitator by phone or in-person at the childcare. The facilitator attended the birth, along with Natalie's partner. Natalie delivered a healthy baby girl.

Mental Health Treatment

Pregnancy, childbirth and parenting are expected to be times of great joy and pride, but pregnancy is accompanied by a myriad of changes and demands. For some women, this is a time of overwhelming and unexpected worries and sadness. About half the women who experience depression after the baby is born have already experienced symptoms during pregnancy.

Many primary care clinics and obstetric practices have found effective ways of including depression screening during regular office visits. Two screening tools are cited most often in the research literature with prenatal multi-ethnic women: Edinburgh Postnatal Depression Scale and the Center for Epidemiological Studies Depression Scale-Revised (Breedlove & Fryzelka, 2011). Routine screenings combined with interview methods can identify women who need additional support with high reliability. Screening is effective at ruling out other medical conditions and at educating women about the symptoms of depression. Many women may not recognize that excessive self-blame, distractibility and inability to sleep can be indicators of a disorder that deserves to be recognized and treated.

Tina called Jeff at work and told him that she wasn't having an easy time and needed him to come home right away. He called Tina's obstetrician, who advised him to take her to the new program developed at the hospital for pregnant and postpartum women experiencing psychiatric symptoms. The program was specifically designed to recognize and treat the overwhelming symptoms of sadness and anxiety often experienced during and after pregnancy. Tina entered day treatment with other women and Jeff got the support he needed to care for his wife and prepare together with her for their baby. While they didn't have the pregnancy they imagined, the guidance, knowledge and treatment Tina received was a lifeline for them and their unborn child.

A woman's obstetrician, primary care physician or mental health provider can treat mild to moderate symptoms of anxiety and depression, when these are recognized. Treatment during pregnancy can take many forms: exercise, psychotherapy, better nutrition and stronger social connections. Treatment for depression does not have to equal medication. Many of us are appropriately cautious about the use of medication during pregnancies. The birth defects caused by thalidomide, a strong sedative given to many women in the 1950s for early pregnancy morning sickness, alerted the world to the possible teratogenic effects of medications during pregnancy.

Women who have severe symptoms of depression; a history of bipolar disorder, major depression or psychosis; or are currently suicidal, should be under psychiatric as well as obstetric care. Antidepressant use in pregnancy has been well evaluated (Yonkers et al, 2009). A Swedish study that included 1.6 million births determined that 19 percent of women experienced depression during pregnancy. Of those that received antidepressants during pregnancy, the researchers found no increased risk of stillbirth or infant death (Stephansson et al, 2013).

A combination of psychotherapy and medication may be recommended and the collaborating physicians can monitor medications that have the smallest risk to the baby. Additionally, breastfeeding shows both preventative and intervention capacities to improve the dyadic relationship and the outcomes for the baby.

It's time to extend the discussion about academic success and emotional readiness for children to include preconception health of women in our communities and the importance of healthy lifestyles, regular medical care and treatment for mental health difficulties and stressful life circumstances during pregnancies.

3

"We can show that if we do a much better job in getting a child ready for school, that child is going to perform much better throughout their life."
Arthur Rolnick

BABY READINESS

The brain what makes us, as humans, amazing.

Once the baby is born, development is transformed into boundless interactive processes that are both interdependent and intradependent. It is the everyday interactions that provide the instructional code for the brain's programming:

- When I cry: what happens?
- When I smile: what happens?
- When I coo: what happens?
- When my diaper is uncomfortable: what happens?
- When I am scared: what happens?
- When I see something new: what happens?
- When I am tired: what happens?

While the baby isn't saying these lines out loud, these are the experiences that are informing the baby's brain and his understanding of relationships, emotions and learning. Early shared interactions—of which there are thousands—can happen while waiting for dinner in the kitchen, changing a diaper or reading a book. These commonplace actions with caring adults tell the baby about his culture and about which tools are essential for the environment into which he was born. Most importantly, these daily actions and interactions with caring adults answer the questions for the baby: "Am I loveable, worthy and important?"

"Brains are built over time."
Jack Shonkoff, MD

BRAIN DEVELOPMENT

Brain development begins a couple of weeks into gestation and continues well into young adulthood, but the first few years of life are a remarkable period of brain development. At birth, the newborn brain is amazingly immature. It contains all of the neurons, but is only a quarter the size of an adult's brain. The most well developed areas of the brain are those responsible for basic biological functions such as breathing and the perception of sensations like touch and hearing. These areas do not require much feedback from the environment but are essential for a baby to gather the information and experience necessary to promote other areas of development. The baby will use the experiences of his or her body, the senses and movements, to begin collecting information, storing memories and developing perceptions about interactions with the world outside of the womb.

Dad watches his 8-week-old son's eyes and mouth and coaches Mario to smile by using a higher-than-normal-pitched voice and forecasting his next action: "You're going to smile. I see you thinking about it. Yes, there it is. You smiley boy!"

FROM THE BABY'S POINT OF VIEW

From the very beginning, Mario learns that his dad is a teacher and cheerleader. As Mario engages in his very first efforts to connect, his dad notices and rejoices in his accomplishments—no matter how small.

Early Experience

The first few years after birth are sensitive periods, during which the brain is primed for specific actions, particularly building points of contacts or synapses between brain cells (Molliver, Kostovic & van der Loos, 1973). By age 2, the toddler's brain will have 100 trillion synaptic connections and weigh three-quarters of the adult brain. As the brain "over prepares" for possibilities, it counts on experience to determine which pathways are most essential to the unique environment in which the child is born. There is actually an overproduction of connection. Those connections that don't get much action are pruned or eliminated to make way for the more frequently used neural highways.

It is as if the brain is preparing for an infinite number of possibilities. And, in many ways it is. The brain is primed to respond to the information it receives for the environment into which the baby is born. For example, a baby has the capacity to learn to speak any world language (Petitto & Marentette, 1991). Scientists have determined that in all of the world languages there are 600 consonants and 200 vowels. Each language has a set of about 40 distinct combinations of these sounds, termed phonemes (Ladefoged, 2001). From the time of birth—and maybe earlier—the baby's brain begins processing the sounds, cadences and accents in her everyday environment. Results of a recent study suggest that newborns are already differentiating sounds of their native tongue from other sounds. Investigators found that newborns will suck on their pacifiers longer when they hear vowel sounds in their mother's language, compared to those of a foreign language (Moon, Lagercrantz & Kuhl, 2013).

> Three-month-old Rubi sits in her baby seat looking at her mom, who is singing to her. Rubi's eyes look intently as her mom sings the phrases from "You Light Up My Life." Mom pauses. Rubi smiles, then begins cooing. Her lips move and her mouth widens as her tone changes. Rubi's eyes are smiling as she mimics the song's rhythm. Mom asks if she knows the words. As mom begins singing again, Rubi joins in. Rubi stops and listens as mom finishes the chorus.

The spoken words in the baby's environment inform and influence the brain development of a baby well in advance of the baby's first word (Kuhl, 2004). Reading, talking and singing with a baby are essential for sturdy brain development. The brain is primed to recognize and reproduce the familiar sounds. By the time a baby is 10 months old, he babbles with sounds that can be differentiated by the spoken language of the parents. We can see this in action, particularly between 10 and 18 months of age. The baby approximates a word such as "daddy" as one phoneme, "da." When the parent responds, "daddy," the brain processes the sounds of the second syllable and the fullness of the word.

The heard phonemes reinforce very specific neuro-circuitry of the individual baby's brain. Linguistic and neurobiological researchers term this process "neural commitment" (Kuhl, 2004). In order to be efficient, the brain commits to improving the proficiencies of the neural circuitry. By 18 months, "da" changes to "Dada go!" These efficiencies mean the brain is preparing to become competent in speaking a particular language.

The neural pathways for sounds and blends not present in the baby's everyday language are not reinforced and eventually will be abandoned. In the wake of efficiencies and the commitment to particular pathways, the brain may actually interfere with reinforcing phonemes that don't conform to the heard language. That is, if the baby processes arbitrary sounds, she may never become proficient in recognizing those most necessary for the spoken language. For example, infants in environments in which Japanese is the primary language can, as very young babies, differentiate between the phonetic r and l. But by 8 to 10 months, the babies begin losing the ability to differentiate these sounds, which are not distinct phonemes in Japanese (Werker et al, 2007).

Language learning is an example of neural development that has a particular period of time, or sensitive period, in which the brain is primed to make certain adjustments that it may be incapable of making easily at other periods of development. The brains of bilingual babies, who are exposed to two languages in social interactions and daily exposures, show more flexibility. The researchers believe that this is a result of daily exposure to the phonemes of two languages.

As older children and adults, we can learn vocabulary of other languages at any age but we have difficulty mastering alternative phonetics and syntax if they were not part of our early learning experience. Those of us who learned a new language after age 5, and particularly after puberty, usually speak the new language with the accent of our native language because we lost the synapses, or neural connections, that would have given us the flexibility to hear and produce the language of a native speaker.

Language development is one of thousands of examples of how brain development is experience-dependent. Because the baby's brain is the most flexible or "plastic" early in development, a baby's environment and distinctive experiences inform and mold the functions of the brain. Through experiences, the neurons previously produced in-utero will be instructed to connect and reinforce. Obviously, a baby can't compute an algebraic equation or determine the consequences of future actions. A lot of experience, growth and foundational development must take place before the child or young adult will have the capacities of these areas of the brain. Early experience builds the scaffolding of normal brain development.

Supporting Neural Development

To improve efficiencies, the brain not only reinforces the important pathways but also makes the speed of the connections faster. The axon of the neuron is the long extension from the cell body that carries the electrical message to the next neuron. In order to improve the speed at which the electrical signal travels, the axon is insulated by a fatty substance, myelin. Most of the myelination of axons happens after birth as primary neural pathways are established. After all, there is no sense in increasing the speed of pathways that will not be used. We can readily see the results of myelination in the regions of the brain responsible for sensory and motor activities as we watch a young baby coordinate her arms and fingers to grasp a ring, or an older baby take his first steps.

The richer the interactions and stimulations, the faster these connections develop and the sturdier the foundation for learning. Children's brains require experience to reinforce brain circuitry. Babies love repetition and routine. Having the same bedtime routine or rereading books helps a baby's brain make connections and build expectations.

The baby's brain development also is dependent on adequate nutrition to ensure proper brain development and myelination, particularly during the first couple of years of life. Breast milk or formula blends the necessary nutrients, fat and calories for healthy brain growth. A high level of fat in a baby's diet is necessary for myelination and iron, which typically we provide in supplements after a baby is 6 months old, ensures that red blood cells are able to fully function and provide the necessary nutrients to the neurons and other cells throughout the body. Appropriate nutrition and adequate calories are essential for proper brain development.

Sometimes development in motor abilities comes in advance of other neurological advancements. For example, babies who are taught sign language may sign the word for "milk" or "more" before they are able to articulate the words. Studies of infants and toddlers show that their interactions with the physical environment accounts for approximately 80 to 90 percent of their waking time; social interactions account for the remaining 10 to 20 percent (White, Kaban, Shapiro & Attanucci, 1977). The baby uses the experiences of his body, senses and movements to start storing memories, perceptions and knowledge about the world. The baby does not require a curriculum to learn; he needs no more—and no less—than consistent, responsive, safe, playful, language-rich engagement.

Signs of Development

Parents quickly learn that a newborn has more neuromuscular control over his head than over his legs and arms. This is the first physical capacity to come "online." Likewise, a baby's ability to be calm and regulate his body while engaging with the world is the first emotional capacity to come online; parents often observe that their baby is better able to attend to a parent's voice and behave more calmly when swaddled.

A unique link between motor, sensory and cognitive development during infancy and toddlerhood is what inspired us at Baby's Space to create intentionally designed childcare spaces. Few early education environments are designed to reflect the specific developmental needs of infants and toddlers. Rather, learning environments are often miniaturized versions of first-grade and kindergarten classrooms filled with small tables, chairs and bookshelves.

FROM THE BABY'S POINT OF VIEW

At 8 months, José sits in the corner of the elevated learning environment. Behind him are mirrored walls; in front, Plexiglas partitions allow him a full view of the room and his teachers. To his left is a carpeted wavy walk that leads to a landing platform before it turns 90 degrees and makes a slow decline towards the floor. To his right, a Plexiglas floor panel, a visual cliff, allows a full view of the crawl-in cave and floor under the panel. When José crosses the Plexi panel, he can dive into a shallow ball pit filled with brightly colored purple, green and yellow balls.

José looks longingly towards the ball pit without moving. His glances at the Plexi bridge are revealing a change in neurodevelopment. José, who up until now has been crawling without hesitation across the see-through floor, is now unsure about crossing. A new ability to perceive depth and to notice the differences between the carpet and Plexi has created a dilemma for José. Working to solve the problem, he scans the play structure, evaluates his options and crawls in the opposite direction, across the wavy walk, down the ramp, over the floor, up the stairs and into the ball pit. It will take him a few weeks to integrate this new perceptual information and to trust the much shorter path over the see-through panel.

At Baby's Space, we use ramps, crawl-in spaces and textures to promote problem-solving and motor development. Mirrored walls allow 360-degree views. We understand that babies learn from their interactions with the physical environment and that this aspect of their development and learning has significance for how babies and their caregivers spend their days.

Babies can tell us a lot about themselves. It takes a while, of course, before they tell us in words, but their body movements, eye contact and facial expressions speak volumes. They tell us when to engage, often when we're changing a diaper, cooing in conversation or spooning in a new food. Neurodevelopmental changes like the development of perception happen each day in the lives of babies and young children.

Through everyday activities repeated over and over, babies' brains learn what neural pathways to reinforce and make speedier. A baby looks under the blanket for the ball that has just been covered, recognizing that the ball, which he can no longer see, still exists. In developmental language, we call this object permanence—the baby knows that something exists even when she can't see it. At about this same time, around 8 to 12 months, the baby makes a fuss after a parent leaves the room. She may use her motor skills to follow after her dad, or to protest loudly. She knows that dad still exists, even when he is out of sight. She uses her resources and strategies to get him back!

A favorite demonstration of neurodevelopment is the recognition of self. The classic study places a red dot on the forehead of a toddler. The child is encouraged to look in a mirror with the idea that if the child recognizes herself in the mirror, she will see the red dot and reach for her forehead.

Proud mother Veronica pulls out her video camera to document her daughter's development. Having just read about the self-recognition study, she uses lipstick to draw a large red dot on 16-month-old Pricilla's forehead. She hoists Pricilla onto the bathroom counter, in front of the bathroom mirror. With a big smile, Pricilla looks into the mirror and pats on the glass. Her glances travel between her mother's reflection in the mirror and her own. She points and babbles. Swings her head from side to side and laughs.

Seeing no indication that her daughter notices the lipstick dot, Veronica uses her finger to smudge a larger mark across Pricilla's forehead. Pricilla looks at her mother and back at the mirror without breaking her smile. She does not seem to notice the dot or the reflected image of herself. Veronica comments about the cute baby in the mirror. Pricilla leans forward and kisses the mirror. She looks to her mother with a huge smile as Veronica reflects, "You're giving that baby a kiss." Pricilla brings her hand to her mouth and kisses her own palm and then gestures her kiss to the mirror image.

At this stage of cognitive development, it is common for children to direct kisses and waves towards themselves. A toddler at this age directly imitates what she sees: a hand waving towards her. The concept of self as separate from her environment has yet to fully emerge. But the developmental transition is not far off.

As parents of 18- to 24-month-olds know, the favorite new word, "no," dominates conversations. Even to questions of delight like, "Do you want ice cream?" the nearly 2-year-old's response may be "No!" What seems like an irrational response is actually an indicator of great neurological growth—the emergence of self. She is now capable of making an independent decision.

Veronica decides to repeat the red dot experiment with Veronica at age 19 months. Standing sturdy on the counter, Veronica holds the lipstick her mother used to make the red dot. "Help," she says as her attempts to get the top off the lipstick container fail. Picking up the soap, she exclaims, "Bubbles," before rubbing the red mark on her forehead.

> ### FROM THE BABY'S POINT OF VIEW
>
> Gone is the sheer delight in seeing the image of another baby in the mirror. Veronica not only knows that the image is her own, she is now working on the important business of getting the red dot off her forehead. Because of new but invisible synaptic connections, she now understands cause and effect and has a sense of purpose and confidence in solving her own problems.

"Me do it" is a commonly heard phrase, which represents an essential and important stage of neurodevelopment and learning readiness. As a 3-year-old, Veronica will begin to develop and communicate narratives of her experiences, reflect on her feelings and put into words what she has learned through her encounters with the world. Developing these skills helps children begin to understand the world beyond their direct experiences. The hallmark of this developmental stage is preschoolers continually asking, "Why?" Answers feed their natural curiosity, broaden their vocabulary and nurture their quest for learning.

Deprivation

Babies' brains are experience-expectant: They respond to touching, talking, looking, rocking, playing, holding and loving. The development of more complex skills is dependent on the quality of the earlier brain processes. When a baby's experiences lack consistent, enriched interactions, when there is neglect or lack of opportunity for interaction, that absence of reinforcement weakens the foundation, creating greater difficulties in future capacity and functioning.

Seven-month-old Brandon spends much of his day in a play saucer in the middle of the living room of his family's small two-bedroom apartment. Both of Brandon's parents have been diagnosed with schizophrenia and receive Social Security Income (SSI). A nurse from the county's adult mental health services visits the parents weekly and oversees their medication management.

By virtue of their mental illness, neither of Brandon's parents is very good at reading his cues and signals. His diaper is changed and he is fed based on a schedule created by Brandon's pediatrician and posted on the refrigerator. During the day, the television blares with the images of violent video games played by his father. The parents have difficulty controlling which friends come in and out of their home. Some people who visit bombard Brandon with attention; others ignore him. Rarely does anyone talk directly to Brandon and no one waits for him to respond.

Both the architecture of brain and the emotional development of infants and toddlers are particularly vulnerable to early life events and disruptions in early caregiving relationships. One of the best current scientific examples we have of this is derived from the studies still being conducted in Romania by a research team led by Charles Nelson and Charles Zeenah (Nelson et al, 2007). After setting up a foster care system for children who otherwise would have lived within an orphanage, the research team assessed and compared the neurobehavioral responses of young children reared in the orphanage, foster homes and biological homes. Their findings, as well as those of others working within orphanages, strongly support the hypothesis that a committed, available and responsive adult and a stimulating environment are central to a young child's physical, neurological and emotional development (Rutter et al, 2010).

The researchers found that, despite adequate nutritional intake, the children living in the orphanage showed marked differences in neuronal activity (event-related potentials or ERPs) and physical development (Parker & Nelson, 2005, Fox, Levitt & Nelson, 2010). In a typical morning at the orphanage, a toddler could expect to spend the first hour of the day sitting on a potty chair with a tray of food on her lap, and to remain that way until all the feeding and toileting of the other 15 children had been completed. After that, hurried along with the other toddlers, she would be escorted into a room with few toys and even fewer adults to find a way to keep herself occupied until the next meal. Under these extraordinary conditions, neuro-imaging shows that her brain underpowers. Nutritionally, she should be on target, but the researchers found that her brain was just not firing up all the way.

These conditions may seem extreme, but there are children within our communities whose physical, social and emotional development is being compromised in a similar manner because of extreme conditions of aberrant caregiving and severe economic hardship. Children share the same basic brain anatomy; experience informs the ways in which our brains process information. Later functioning is dependent on the basic cognitive processes and sensory perceptual systems established in early childhood (Tierney & Nelson, 2009). Experiences impact the architecture of the brain that will be responsible for complex thinking, reasoning, planning and self-control, capacities that may not be apparent until adolescence or early adulthood, when the brain reaches mature functioning. In essence, the brain is ordered in development and relies on a sturdy foundation. While much of brain development takes a full 20 years to develop, the later and more complex processes are built on the foundation set during infancy and toddlerhood.

*"Attachment is an integral part of human
nature from cradle to grave."*
John Bowlby. MD

RELATIONSHIP EXPECTANT

The good news is that there are many, many things parents, caregivers and communities can do to support early brain development and later competencies. Healthy brain development depends on responsive and consistent relationships in environments that are safe enough to allow learning and exploration (Swain, Lorberbaum, Kose, & Strathearn, 2007). The key is consistent, sensitive and responsive relationships created between the baby her primary caring adults.

Babies are completely dependent on adults, and preprogrammed to form powerful connections with their parents and others who care for them. They are relationship expectant. Obviously babies can't survive without adults to provide for their basic needs and to protect them, but just as important, adults translate the information necessary for brain development. For example, talking and singing to babies while changing diapers or feeding gives them examples of language.

From birth, or perhaps even before, a child has the nascent skills to form and maintain relationships. A newborn remembers his mother's voice from prenatal exposure, for example, and will show a preference for her voice over a stranger's. A newborn staring into his dad's face, an older infant rounding her lips into an "o" as dad coos and mirrors back her expression, an adult responding to a toddler asking to be pushed on a swing... all of these are responsive and engaged parent-child interactions.

In an alert state, babies will imitate.

One-hour-old 's Manny's head is cradled by his father's hand. His face, still ruddy from delivery, is directed towards his dad's. With the beeping of monitors and the cry of another newborn in the background, Manny's father announces that they are going to play the tongue sticking out game. Manny struggles to find his father's face, first opening his mouth and then his eyes.

As his Manny's eyes fix on his face, dad sticks out his tongue and waits. Manny's closed lips pucker. Bubbles begin forming in the seam, as his tongue creates a wave of movement inside of his mouth. The intensity of his efforts is clearly visible. His mouth opens. A flat tongue thrusts in and out. Then a sharply pointed tongue emerges. One hour old, Manny notices and imitates.

With the tender sound of dad's voice, Manny's face and mouth move with rhythm and interest. Studies show that parents who share in the discoveries of their newborn's capacities demonstrate more sensitivity at 11 months and stronger engagement at one year. Clearly, from Manny's first breath, he is looking for and dependent on relationships, interactions and experiences (Brazelton, 1992).

In the beginning, Manny's emotional needs are simple: He needs his caregivers to show up, physically and emotionally. This is good news for his overwhelmed and sleep-deprived parents. These opportunities to foster trust and show affection present themselves constantly in ordinary moments like changing a diaper, nursing and playing patty-cake. Showing up doesn't require a huge bag of tricks.

Babies are born with the growing ability to express the internal activities of their brains; they can communicate what they feel, what they think and how they learn. These early expressions of emotions, desires and distress motivate the development of imitative and reciprocal relations with their adult caregivers. The baby's internal drive to connect with his caring adults and their responses helps create the optimal environment for healthy development.

Luckily, tired moms and dads get a benefit too: Responding to the cues of their babies and engaging in nurturing skin-to-skin interactions like hugging and breastfeeding increases parents' "cuddle hormone," oxytocin. Increases in this particular hormone—known for pleasurable feelings of closeness and intimacy—are the well-deserved reward for the all-consuming job of sensitive and responsive parenting. The emergence of the social smile at about 3 or 4 months of age is just the boost that new parents need as the endorphins from childbirth begin to wear off and sleep deprivation begins to take a toll.

Babies come biologically equipped with characteristics and behaviors that increase the likelihood of attracting good quality care and forming a secure attachment with at least one caregiver (Bowlby, 1969/1982). Nature provides babies with round heads, plump cheeks and engaging eyes that elicit endearing remarks and affirming comments from family and strangers alike. A baby smiles, babbles and cries to attract attention from the caring adults around her. In so doing, she elicits positive and supportive responses from adults. Playing peek-a-boo and smiling at an attractive and responsive baby is a win-win for both baby and adult.

> Manny, now a robust 5-month-old, sits in his bouncing seat watching his mom as she prepares the evening meal. Playing occasionally with the toy bar in front of him and cooing at his mom, he seems content and relaxed, at least for the time being. Five minutes later, Manny starts making the first sounds of displeasure. His mother smiles and with a sing-song voice lets Manny know that she hears him, she loves him and that she is almost done cooking dinner. At the sound of his mother's voice, Manny smiles, settles and plays again with his toys. Within a few minutes, the pattern repeats and, while returning to play, Manny begins to suck on his fingers. Finally, no longer able to comfort himself, Manny's whimper becomes a wail. Knowing that the sound of her voice will no longer be enough to console him, Manny's mom retrieves him from his seat. Manny immediately stops crying and smiles at mom.

FROM THE BABY'S POINT OF VIEW

Through these everyday interactions, Manny learns emotional regulation. He practices entertaining himself and waiting for his mom to finish cooking. When he fusses, his mom helps him find new ways of being entertained: listening to her voice, reengaging with his toys. But when boredom or hunger overtake his ability to manage on his own, a mere change in the tone or frequency brings his mother's added attention. He learns just how upset he needs to get to gain the necessary attention from his parent. His smile helps seal the deal—yep, a hug from mom is just what he needs.

Consistent experiences such as this, while seeming ordinary and perhaps unremarkable, teach Manny valuable lessons about his own capacity to attend and regulate his experience, engage in a two-way relationship and communicate back and forth with his mom. Through everyday experiences, Manny develops the capacities that allow him to become an even more effective communicator and to manage small stresses on his own. A responsive and sensitive caregiver helps a very young child manage daily challenges and, in gradual steps, to learn a variety of skills, including how to soothe himself and meet or delay his own needs. When his limited strategies are exhausted, he has learned to rely on mom to come to his aid.

Learning through parents' consistent responses, he cries, smiles or gains new skills. Countless ordinary experiences with mom or dad help a baby learn the pleasure, comfort and security of relationships. He smiles when the parent walks into the room and seeks reassurance when wary. He's come to expect her help with the myriad of daily experiences that he's too young to handle by himself.

Between 6 months and 2 years, we can really see how a baby begins to organize his behaviors to maintain engagement with his primary caregivers. Many practitioners use dancing to describe the interconnected nature of the attachment relationship: As one partner leads, the other follows. If the baby does something, the parent reacts, which then impacts the baby's next action. In a smooth flow of movements and interactions that respond to changes in tempo, directions and the nuances of intimacy, the dyad dances.

Everyday experiences like Manny's interaction with his parents help him understand his connection with others. As Manny grows and matures, so will his capacity to experience, manage and express a broader and more distinct range of emotions; to engage in problem solving and imaginative play expressing emotions; and to make logical connections. The caring adults who surround him will act as cheerleaders, marvel at his accomplishments and revise their expectations for his developing capacities in attention, relationship building and communication.

Children carry forward what they learn during middle-of-the-night feedings, afternoons at the park and everyday moments of love and attention as they move further and further out from their primary relationships and into the world. Children with a sense of security and basic trust in relationships bring this perspective with them into new relationships and situations.

Lilly, 17 months old, looks into the glass aquarium at the local zoo, watching two otters swimming and playing right at her own eye level. She reaches toward them, stomping her feet and squealing in delight. Her finger points to the otters as she glances back at her dad on her left. Looking right, Lilly notices a lighted display. She looks at the otter again, then back at the display. With confidence, Lilly walks toward the display, her pointing finger leading the way. She finds the picture of the otter on the lighted board, looks at the otter in the tank, glances back at her father, and then, once again, looks at the display picture. She's made the connection: The picture of the otter and the live, swimming otter are related. Exuberant at her discovery, Lilly runs back and forth between the aquarium and the display. Her confidence and excitement about learning is clear (Rose, 2012b).

A secure, flexible and trusting relationship with a primary caregiver prepares infants and toddlers for academic and social competence. Lilly's thoughtful, engaged parents are helping her reach her full potential by following her interests, encouraging play, and providing a secure environment filled with opportunities for learning. As Lilly matures, she will be able to use words as well as gestures to communicate her discoveries. Her interest in the world will broaden beyond the simple labeling of objects to the creation of themes and storylines. She will be able to imagine through dress-up that she is an otter and represent experiences from the zoo in her play, along with other real-life episodes and whimsical ideas. By developing and communicating narratives of her experiences, Lilly will be able to reflect on her feelings, put into words what she has learned through her encounters and share her thoughts with others.

Manny and Lilly need no more—and no less—than consistent, sensitive and responsive caring adults who provided safe, playful and language-rich environments. It's no accident that babies' needs start out simple (food, diaper changes, cuddling) and become more complex as their parents get smarter. We learn about sitting up and toilet training as our babies do. When adults provide consistent, sensitive and responsive care to infants and toddlers, children learn to trust others.

Listening attentively to the baby, showing affection and creating environments in which the interests and experiences of children are valued are activities that support healthy relationships. Babies succeed when caring adults give them consistent love and support with opportunities for engagement and learning. Toddlers succeed when their loving adults provide enough structure to allow them to be big and little at the same time and help them find ways to balance their big emotions. Preschoolers succeed when they receive the guidance, support and encouragement to try new things, repeat their accomplishments and expand their skills learned through trusted relationships to new friends. Through these early relationships, children gain a sense of belonging and competence.

We believe that providing the best start to life for a baby is the most important job for both parents and the community. Why? Because our intuition and research shows that when a strong foundation supports a healthy, happy baby, he is most likely to succeed in school and relationships—and as a citizen of the world.

Science of Relationships

Psychologist and attachment theory pioneer John Bowlby described the connectedness that develops during infancy between a baby and his caregiver. He formed his theory of attachment by studying abandoned and homeless children after World War II. He was particularly interested in the importance of caring, consistent and nurturing relationships for children between the ages of 6 months and 2 years, the period when children's reactions to separations change. Their cognitive abilities develop, allowing them to realize that people and objects exist even when out of sight, and that their own actions can produce consequences.

In a theoretical trilogy, Bowlby outlined attachment theory as the process by which infants become attached to those primary caregivers who are sensitive, responsive and consistently available. He developed the concept of the secure base of the primary caregiver; as babies become more mobile and explore their surroundings, they maintain contact with this base. Attachment behaviors are most salient between the ages of 6 and 25 months, when children's survival, development and cognitive capacities are most intricately linked to their interactions with others.

Bowlby described the attachment process by which an infant seeks connectedness and protection. There were four primary characteristics that differentiated the relationship a child had with his parent or primary caregiver. The child wants to be close and connected; sees the parent as a safe haven, someone who provides comfort; feels secure to explore when the parent is present, using the parent as a secure base; and is distressed (or anxious) when not with the parent or another attachment figure. Bowlby maintained that infants and toddlers engage in a variety of predictable behaviors that are linked to the critical nature of their connection with the adults who care for them. A sensitive, responsive and consistent parent-child relationship helps the child build a sense of self that includes self worth, empathy and empowerment. The attachment with the parent provides a model for future relationships and expectations.

Bowlby's attachment theory has been expanded and tested in many ways. Mary Ainsworth and her colleagues used attachment theory and these predictable behaviors to study the differences in the ways infants responded to their primary caregivers and the qualities of their interactions. She and her colleagues studied attachment in the context of separation (Ainsworth, 1967). They developed the Ainsworth's Strange Situation Procedure, which measures the quality of parent-infant attachment in a laboratory setting by observing, in a standardized way, relatively common separation and reunion events between young children and their primary caregivers.

FROM THE BABY'S POINT OF VIEW

Belinda loves her mom and certainly does not like that her mom left her with someone who she does not know. She does not want the friendly stranger to comfort her and is not interested in playing with the toys. She waits for her mother to return because she knows her mom will be back, just like she said. Once reunited, she hugs her mom for reassurance and love. Brushing off the separation with a sigh, she begins to play again.

Belinda, 14 months old, watches as a stranger walks into the room where she and her mother have been playing. The friendly stranger smiles and sits on a chair not far from where Belinda's mother is filling out paperwork. Belinda sits on the floor between the two adults and continues to place plastic blocks into a container. Glancing at the stranger, Belinda offers her a plastic block. Within a few minutes of the stranger entering, Belinda's mom rises from her chair and leaves the room. Mom reassures her daughter that she will be right back. Belinda follows her mother to the door, crying in protest. The stranger offers a toy to Belinda and picks her up. While willing to be held, Belinda places her arms between her body and the shoulder of the stranger and continues to cry. She signals that she wants to be placed on the floor, then sits among the toys, fingering the blocks with her head down.

When Belinda hears a rattle behind the door where her mother disappeared, she looks up at the stranger and back to the door. Her mother reappears. She takes a deep breath and crawls to her mother. Once in her mother's arms, she accepts the toy offered and again plays with the same enthusiasm she showed before the separation.

Ainsworth defined this pattern as "secure attachment." The idea is that the laboratory setting elicits patterns of interactions between the dyad that have been well grooved by thousands of shared everyday moments. The child's behavior indicates her ability to use the parent as a secure base from which to explore the world and to solicit and receive comfort when stressed. In these experiments, Ainsworth and other researchers have found that babies who enjoy secure parent-child relationships also have adaptive flexibility (Sroufe, Egeland, Carlson, & Collins, 2005). Securely attached children develop an image of themselves as powerful, that they have the capacities to influence social interactions (Tronik, 2012). They are both dependent upon the relationship and an active contributor to the care received.

Development of Empathy

By expressing love, acknowledging feelings and experiences and providing a protective presence while children explore their environments, parents model the confidence, encouragement and optimism that support early development As children grow, they develop strong foundations and display more resilience when parenting practices encourage autonomy, offer effective discipline, support adjustments to cope with financial realities and provide links to the community and social networks (Sroufe, Egeland, Carlson & Collins, 2005). When children are shown empathy, understanding and competence, they are able to translate these capacities into new settings and experiences.

Children who begin life with a sense of security and basic trust in relationships bring this perspective with them into new relationships and situations. We call this a secure attachment. For these children, their foundations for relationships are that adults who care for them can be trusted and that they themselves are competent, important and loveable. Substantial research indicates that early supportive and responsive care results in children who will have positive regard for themselves and others and possess a prototype for relationships based on this foundation of security (National Institute of Child Health and Human Development [NICHD] Early Child Care Research Network, 1997; Sroufe, Egeland, Carlson, & Collins, 2005).

Empathy is an expression of the learned art of relating and of a coordinated emotional regulation system (Sroufe & Fleeson, 1986). Children learn that when one person is in need, another person responds with kindness and sensitivity. Preschool children with secure attachment relationships are more likely to show empathy for a hurt playmate by expressing concern and getting a teacher to help (Waters, Wippman & Sroufe, 1979; Troy & Sroufe, 1987).

Owen has been trying to learn to ride his bike for three weeks. While so discouraged by his inability to pedal that he told his dad that he should sell his bike, he agrees to try one more time. Success!

Wanting to capture the moment of accomplishment, Owen's dad grabs his camera phone and asks Owen how he feels.

"I feel happy of myself."

The father responds, "I feel happy of yourself, too."

Owen is asked to give advice to other kids learning to ride their bikes and says: "Everybody, I know you can believe in yourself. If you believe in yourself, you will know how to ride a bike. If you don't, you just keep practicing."

It is clear by Owen's own statements that his parents followed his interest, encouraged his learning and provided a nurturing and supportive environment. Dad's response to his son's confidence shows how deep is his affection and support. "I feel happy of yourself, too." Rather than correcting Owen's grammar, dad reaffirmed his son's experience and confidence.

In the development of empathy, when children are held to an expectation to see from the perspective of others, they begin to believe in their capacities to benefit their families, siblings and community. There is an amplification of their connectedness to others. Owen's dad's affirmation of his son's success is followed with a belief that his son's learning has greater purpose. His dad and expects that Owen's own experience can and will benefit others. At 5 years old, Owen is asked to think of others, to translate the support he has received.

FROM THE BABY'S POINT OF VIEW

Owen responds with thoughtful preparation when his dad asks, "Do you have any words of wisdom for the other kids trying to learn to ride their bikes?" Reciting the lessons that he clearly learned from the reassuring presence and encouragement of his parents, Owen places himself in the shoes of other 5-year-olds: "Everybody, I know you can believe in yourself. If you believe in yourself, you will know how to ride a bike. If you don't, you just keep practicing."

On the first day of kindergarten, Owen's backpack for success will include confidence, interest in learning and a motivation to connect with others. We can imagine a future kindergarten teacher's delight in Owen's self-assurance, enthusiasm and empathy. Teachers tend to treat children with secure histories with greater affection, respect and matter-of-fact approaches. In middle childhood, when the hallmark of emotional health is involvement with friends, children who have a confident sense of how relationships work are less likely to isolate themselves (Sroufe, Egeland, Carlson & Collins, 2005). Good relationships produce good relationships. Feeling cared for and nurtured creates the opportunity to care for others and cultivates empathy (Trevarthen & Aitken, 1994).

Children who have a secure relationship with their parents enter kindergarten with confidence, fully capable of building and sustaining relationships with teachers and handling the everyday challenges on the playground. They bring with them an understanding that others can be trusted and that they themselves are competent, important and loveable. They are easily engaged and intrigued by learning and discovery in the classroom (Pianta, Cox, & Snow, 2007). Securely attached children have a sense of belonging and responsibility to their own learning and the well-being of their fellow students. They experience fewer behavioral problems and have an easier time developing positive relationships with peers, teachers and others.

Third-graders who have had loving, responsive early experiences achieve higher math scores than those who have not (Sroufe, Egeland, Carlson & Collins, 2005). It is not that loving relationships literally make children smarter; rather, these relationships build a child's self-confidence, communication skills and ability to ask for help. Learning—and life—is easier when you have these tools in your toolbox. Imagine being a third-grader and getting stuck on a math problem. Children with confidence turn to a neighbor or seek help from a teacher and persist until they meet academic challenges.

A model for relationships

Securely attached children have a preference for relationships that are consistent, reliable, sensitive and nurturing. The series of dance steps we learned through our experiences of being parented become the playbook for future relationships. This playbook—or, as attachment theorists call it, internal working model for relationships—guides how we think of ourselves in relation to others. This working model is relatively stable across our lifespan. It's fortified by successful relationships with teachers and peers and, eventually, romantic relationships.

We seek out relationships that mirror the qualities of our earliest relationships with their parents—an intergenerational transmission of the ways in which relationships are formed and maintained. Adolescents who have a model of themselves as loving and loveable see themselves as socially competent, trusting, expressive and able to be assertive in dating and forming friendships (Cassidy & Shaver, 2008; Sroufe, Egeland, Carlson & Collins, 2005). When their romantic partners disclose information about themselves, teens with secure histories are more responsive and empathic. College dating couples who feel satisfaction and trust are supportive of each other and are comfortable with commitment.

Hazan and Shaver (1987) found that the playbook for successful romantic relationships is similar to that of secure parent-infant attachment relationships. They found that successful romantic relationships engaged in the following behaviors:
- Feel safe when the other is nearby and responsive.
- Engage in close, intimate, body contact.
- Feel insecure when the other is inaccessible.
- Share discoveries with one another.
- Play with one another's facial features.
- Exhibit a mutual fascination and preoccupation with one another.
- Engage in "baby talk."

While the primary caregiving relationship usually develops between parents and their baby, and parents are certainly the child's first teacher, parents aren't the only significant relationships in the baby's life. A baby will learn from and form significant relationships with other caring adults, such as grandparents and teachers. A child learns to rely on an intimate team of caring adults. As Manny, Lilly and Owen develop and grow, they will come in contact with others and learn how to get along with and care for others based on experiences with a cadre of caring adults. Each child will translate all of these early experiences into an internal working model that he or she will use in daily life. The security and encouragement they received will influence their abilities to manage the challenges arise and guide their future connections with friends, co-workers, lovers and community.

"I am beautiful, are I?"
3-year-old

MENTAL HEALTH

Margaret Mahler and other an early attachment theorist, describes the period of the first year and the process of attachment as the transformation of the infant from a physiological being to a psychological being (Mahler, Pine & Bergman, 1975). A parent-infant partnership is not only essential in helping the infant develop a sense of trust and self-confidence but also in helping the developing capacities regulate a myriad of internal and external experiences. A parent is there to overcome the baby's developmental limitations. For example, a baby has difficulty regulating his body temperature or sleeping through the night. An interactive loop develops a dyadic regulatory process that steers by the baby's signals and influenced by caregivers responses.

On a beautiful spring day, Jana places her 6 month-old son Matt on a blanket she placed on the lawn outside of their home. Matt seems amused by the toys spread on the blanket and Jana is happy to be outside enjoying the sunshine. A loud bark from a dog in the neighbor's yard startles Matt and he begins to fuss. Jana responds with reassurance "Did you hear that dog? I am right here." Matt looks at his mom, smiles and goes back to playing with the toys before him. At the sound of another bark, Matt furrows his brow and again fusses, this time with more agitation. Jana's voice is quick and sympathetic as she picks him up reassuring him: "It is okay. It is just a doggie." She carries Matt over to where they can see the dog wagging his tail on the other side of the fence. Jana talks to Matt about the dog and lets him watch the dog from the safety of her arms.

This familiar scene emphasizes that consistent experiences such as this teach Matt valuable lessons. What happens when an experience is beyond his control or understanding? How upset does he need to get? Through everyday experiences, Matt develops the capacities that allow him to become an even more effective communicator and manage small stresses on his own. He learns that when he reaches the point when he is no longer able to manage his own emotional experience, he can count on his mom to help him.

FROM THE BABY'S POINT OF VIEW

At six months of age, almost every interaction provides an opportunity for discovery. Touching the grass, hearing the dog bark, and feeling the warmth of the sun on his face are all new experiences for Matt. Even the commonly heard bark of the neighborhood dog is something new for Matt and his emerging abilities. His mother's gentle guidance and calm body helps him connect the noise to the dog while providing reassurance as he gets to know his four-legged neighbor.

Not only does the parent-child relationship help Matt manage those challenges that he is too young to effectively conquer on his own, it also helps him translate his physical, sensory, and emotional experiences into language. "Too hot!" says mom as she blows on his spoonful of food. "So mad," she says as her toddler flays on the floor after being told no more cookies. "You did it," she remarks as Matt places the fifth block on the tower she is supporting from the bottom.

If a child can affectively organize himself and his world by age 2, he's built for social, academic and emotional success. He'll likely move through his world confident in his own abilities and in the availability and support of others. As Matt grows and matures, so will his capacity to experience, manage, and express a broader and more distinct range of emotions, learning and relationships.

> Three-year-old Matt is invited to play at his new friend Teddy's house. Matt's mom stays for a few minutes to help him get use to his new surroundings and leaves Teddy's mom with her telephone number. After his mom leaves, Matt stands still for several minutes. The tears that welled in his eyes begin to spill on the floor. Teddy's mom reassures Matt that his mom will be back and that they have lots of fun toys at their house. Matt turns to her and says, "It's okay. My eyes are just watering."

Babies are born with the ability to express the internal activities of their brains; they can communicate what they feel, what they think and how they learn. These early expressions of emotions, desires and distress motivate the development of imitative and reciprocal relations with their adult caregivers. The baby's growing abilities to attend and regulate allow him to tolerate the frustrations of learning new skills like dropping a block through a hole in a shape sorter, pulling on a sock or riding a bike.

The abilities to express and manage a broader and more distinct range of emotions, engage in problem solving, express emotions during imaginative play and make logical connections grow with time. Play is where children learn the most about their abilities to negotiate, express thoughts and feelings and begin making logical connections. Developing these kinds of skills help children begin to develop an understanding of the world beyond their direct experiences.

Defining Mental Health in Young Children

Mental = the processes of the mind. Health = soundness and well-being.

Capturing the importance of early experience and regulation, ZERO TO THREE, a national nonprofit organization promoting the healthy development of infants and toddlers, defines infant mental health in terms of a child's developing capacity of the child from birth to 3 to:

• Form close and secure interpersonal relationships.

- Experience, regulate and express emotions.
- Explore the environment and learn.

All within the context of family, community and cultural expectations for young children (Parlakian & Seibel, 2002).

What stands out about this definition is that it translates across the age ranges and can be seen in a 2-month-old, 14-month-old or 3-year-old and is easily understood. By using this definition, parents, policymakers and professionals can begin to see how early childhood mental health sets the stage for healthy relationships, school readiness and the abilities to manage the joys and challenges of childhood. The first few years of life are a time of rapid growth and development that take place within the context of intimate relationships informed by parental, cultural and community experiences, expectations and capacities.

Mental Health Capacities

After observing children and studying development for more than a quarter of a decade, Stanley Greenspan identified six developing experiences or capacities determined to be central to mental health (Greenspan, 1999). These capacities and social functions develop in the context of relationships and are aligned with the growth of the brain's capacities. Each capacity emerges and progresses in line with physical, neurological and social growth. And, while each of the capacities comes on-line in a predictable sequence, the subsequent development of each capacity is interdependent and viewed as essential for all later development of the mind and well-being.

Attention and regulation

The very first capacity, which is evident even in a newborn, is the ability to be calm and to regulate an interest in the world. The newborn, such as in the anecdote about sticking out his tongue, notices what is going on in her world when attentive and relaxed. She gradually builds a repertoire of knowledge based on sensory experiences. Each day she tastes, smells, sees and touches things that are familiar and unfamiliar. Development allows her to sustain attention for longer and longer periods, from a brief moment as a newborn who only holds eye contact for a few seconds to more elaborate and continuous interactions as a toddler. To effectively learn, a child needs to be able to attend and sustain interactions—to look and listen—without over- or under-reacting to the environment (ZTT, 2005).

We see this simultaneous, mutually dependent growth of physical and emotional capacities at all stages of a child's development. In the earliest weeks of life, a baby practices head control and eye contact. The swaddled baby works to focus his attention on a parent's lips as she is talking to him. Over time, he will gain control more and more control over his movements and be able to sustain attention for longer periods of time, allowing him to sustain interest in mouthing a toy and later in trying to fit a block into various holes in a shape sorter. A toddler will persist in stacking two blocks.

> Dad asks two-year-old Jayden to draw a picture on the computer pad that he is holding. Jayden responds in a cooperative tone, "Nope." Knowing that his son really meant to say yes, Dad restates his request. Jayden looks at the icons on the computer pad and says, "Big dinosaur." Then, his fingers move towards the wrong icon. Dad redirects. Jayden responds, "Okay." He taps on the correct icon and with delight says, "Here it is."

In preschool, Jayden will bring the same persistence to the task of holding a pair of scissors and cutting a circle out of construction paper. On the trajectory of normal child development, a child's maturing motor abilities integrate seamlessly with simultaneously developing abilities to maintain focus and regulate.

Forming close relationships

Not far behind attention and regulation is the capacity to form relationships with others, which is first evidenced by the social smile.

While there will be bonding, the initial "falling in love" stage of the parent-child relationship is a one-way interaction from parent to child. Around 4 to 6 months of age, we see the baby's ability to engage others in warm interactions take hold. At this point, the baby is an active participant in the parent-infant attachment relationship, seeking pleasure, comfort and security from caring adults.

> Eight-month-old Gabriella sits on the floor playing with her mom. She smiles as she babbles in conversation. Mom announces that daddy is home. While still out of sight, she hears her dad say "Hi sweetie." Gabriella's mouth rounds and her eyes widen. Once she sees him, she begins rocking forward towards her dad, waving her arms for him to pick her up. Dad makes a big kiss sound that Gabriella imitates.

The excitement in the relationship is visible when dad returns from a day at work and her baby flaps his arms and smiles in delight at his presence. These early relationship capacities set the stage for the child to be affectively engaged in relationships with grandparents, teachers, and peers.

Babies learn empathy and to care for others based on their earliest experiences in forming relationships. Children who can count on their parents when they are fussy, hungry, or frustrated overtime learn how to engage in relationships and to help others. Learning to share, to identify and appreciate similarities and differences, and to see from the perspective of others are part of forming secure and supportive relationships.

Two-way communication

As a newborn, a cry in response to hunger or discomfort may be undifferentiated and the baby is completely dependent on adults to figure out the appropriate response. Beginning in tandem with relationships skills, the baby becomes adept at signaling, using verbal and nonverbal strategies to communicate desires, experiences, thoughts and feelings. We know from research on sign language that a baby has thoughts to communicate well before he has verbal language skills. An infant or toddler may use pointing and gestures to engage in a back-and-forth conversation.

Babies and parents are designed to be receptive to each other's cues and to adapt to each other's signals. Being able to purposefully express intention occurs well in advance of verbal language. In a baby's first few months, she learns that her signals result in actions and reactions from others. A simple cry in the middle of the night gets mom's attention. A little gurgle causes dad to echo a response. The more sensitively and quickly parents respond to their baby's crying communications, the more quickly a baby learns patterns of non-crying communication.

A recent study involving one hundred twenty children ages 18 to 48 months determined that language skills and emotional regulation are closely connected (Roben, Cole, & Armstrong, 2012). The children were asked to wait eight minutes before opening a gift placed before them. Children with more well-developed language skills were more likely to seek support and use distraction to tolerate the delay. Children whose language was less developed were more likely to express anger and have difficulty withstanding the delay.

Solving problems with a sense of self

During the second year, with the emergence of a baby seeing herself as an independent person, the emergence of problem solving—that is, "how do I get what I want?"—is clear. This is a charming new capacity for developmentalists and a challenging new capacity for parents and teachers. The emergence of this capacity changes the nature of the parent-child relationship from a fluid dance in which each partner takes a turn to interactions in which a toddler wants as many turns as possible and has a variety of strategies to get them. A structured and predictable environment in which the child has the ability to express choice within carefully controlled options nurtures this capacity.

At fourteen months of age, Brianna knows what she wants
– the can of soda pop that mom has placed in the middle
of the round coffee table. Reaching towards the middle
of the table, the pop can is inches from Brianna's reach.
She rounds the table, trying without success from every
angle. Finding a napkin on the table, Brianna pushes the
napkin towards the can, trying again from multiple sides of
the round table. She indicates her frustration with a short
grunt and look towards mom. Not wanting to give up,
Brianna spots a pillow and places it on the floor. Standing
on the pillow, she successfully hoists her body onto the
coffee table and thrusts her outstretched arm towards the
soda pop.

Consistent and reliable limits can also help a young child develop
problem-solving skills. All of us do better when we know the rules, but
toddlers in particular feel safer when they know someone is helping
them set limits. It will always be a toddler's job to ask for more—and
a parent's job to set the boundaries. A toddler and preschooler do
better when adults set the limits. Think "red cup-blue cup." The child
gets to choose the color, the adult controls that he uses a cup. Or,
"All done books," can be a helpful phrase when the toddler wants to
delay bedtime by asking to read one more book. Our goal is for the
child to use his problem-solving skills successfully while maintaining
appropriate reactions to limits. The capacity to both create solutions
and accept limitations is essential for school success.

Expression of thoughts and feelings

Very young children, especially 2- and 3-year-olds, are learning
how to manage and express their emotions. They experience shining
moments of success and dismal failures. The key thing for adults to
remember is that the child really is constantly building these skills—
even if it's not obvious yet to the rest of us. He's in the process
of gaining a broader and more appropriate range of expression

and management strategies. Part of this process is learning words to express their feelings. Teaching children appropriate responses through demonstration can be really helpful. Before the child hits, for example, tell him, "Say, 'that's mine' or 'that makes me mad.'"

> Chin's family had a rule against violent action figures. Playing by himself, Chin let his parents know what he thought about the rule. They overheard the plastic tiger in his left hand "tell" the plastic tiger in his right hand, "My mommy won't buy me Ninja Turtle." (His parents bought him the action figures—but removed the swords.)

Using play to project experiences, thoughts and feelings helps children explore their intentions and connections to others. A child begins to develop ideas and elaborate on his needs by creating symbolic images. If the child role-plays "dad," he can begin to see from another's perspective and to work out related emotional experiences—particularly about power and control. A child begins to identify with characters and storylines from books and movies to try on these new roles and the associated emotions.

Logical linkages of emotions and ideas

The final capacity emerges as the preschool child begins to make connections between actions and creates narratives with beginnings, middles and ends. Emotional experiences now have context and the child can produce cause thinking: "He was mean to me, so I hit him. He never lets me play in his room." Emotional experiences have moved beyond labeling and can be applied to others. At this age, children begin to act on their feelings of empathy and understanding of other's perspectives. "Saying sorry" must include the "what" the child did to cause the other person's pain. "Sorry, Jack, for hitting you and making you cry." Helping children interpret and rehearse their understanding of other's experiences and feelings can benefit the development of this capacity, allowing for children to express empathy.

Teaching children to recognize the full array of feelings (e.g. embarrassed or frustrated) and identify situations in which those feelings might arise supports logical linkages. Helping children to develop scripts and problem-solving strategies for imagined scenarios lets them understand how they and others experience emotions and express feelings. "If Johnny's pencil broke, how would he feel? What should he do? What could his friend do?"

The National Scientific Council on the Developing Child (2007) concludes: "Emotional well-being, social competence and cognitive abilities together are the bricks and mortar that comprise the foundation of human development" This is the time to shout from the rooftops and become steadfast in our conviction that a secure, flexible and trusting relationship with the primary caregiver is the single most important predictor of a child's academic and social competence, for the development of empathy and for creating a model of supportive and trusting future relationships.

4

"We reinvented family life in the twentieth century
but never wrote a user's manual."
William Doherty, PhD

PARENT READINESS

Collectively, parents are the village. Yet, we operate in isolation and receive little or no formal training or coaching. For most of us, our own experiences of being parented and teenage stints babysitting the neighbor's children, coupled with reading a few parenting books accounts for our formal education and internship experiences. Moreover, our on-the-job training is void of instructions or any user-friendly operating systems.

Parenting is challenging. Navigating typical developmental milestones, decisions around potty training and sleeping arrangements, and finding a consistent caregiving team challenge the most prepared of parents. For those of us whose own experiences of being parented were less than stellar, we must learn new patterns of interactions and what it means to be a consistent and sensitive parent.

Paramount must be a dedication to educating our heads and hearts about the critical nature of our roles as parents. Young children do best when: their parents are fully committed as nurturers, protectors and disciplinarians; continue to educate themselves about child development; find networks for social and parenting support; learn effective ways to manage stress; and are not burdened by inadequate basic needs.

Parent education programs, home visiting and early childhood programs can reinforce and enhance the essential elements of healthy parent-child relationships and help keep the focus on the parent's central role in protecting and supporting the young child. With support, guidance, and knowledge, parents can chaperon their child's abilities to sustain meaningful and satisfying relationships, develop empathy and understanding for others, and learn to manage life's daily ups and downs.

"The hand that rocks the cradle rarely controls the world.
But the voice that sings the lullabies and barks cautionary
messages in the first years of life provides critical information
about the social niche into which the child has been born."

Sarah Blaffer Hrdy, PhD

LEARNING TO PARENT

Providing the best start to life for a baby is the most important job for both parents and the community. Our intuition and research show that when a strong foundation supports a healthy, happy baby, he is most likely to succeed in school and relationships—and as a citizen of the world. In fact, we can say that the development of the hearts, souls and minds of babies is relationship-dependent, requiring close, sensitive and consistent connections with a few caring adults. Parents who provide a steady stream of ordinary, predictable interactions each day safeguard their baby's development.

Our ideas about parenting are both knowingly and circuitously influenced by our personal experiences as children, as well as by all of the cultural information we come in contact with on a daily, if not hourly, basis. We all carry preconceived notions of parenthood—of what a mother and father should be, how she should approach her role and handle his responsibilities. We all share the experience of having been babies, which means that we share the experience of being parented—and attached. And, who doesn't know how to be a parent?

Traditionally, extended family and tribal living arrangements may have filled in the gaps in knowledge and abilities for young and unskilled parents. Many cultural practices, in the past and today, safeguarded babies while attending to mothers' needs for rest and families' needs for connections to communities. Culture helps define which child behaviors require attention as well as the appropriate responses by the parent to the child's attempts at communication and regulation. These experiences get incorporated into our daily interactions and expectations of ourselves as parents. Advice and parenting partners were built into daily life, with support from family members and/or the community, so no formal parenting education was needed.

Becoming a parent is an ancient, natural phenomenon, yet many of us feel ill equipped for the role. Today, many parents are raising families with greater distance and isolation from family and community. Many parents of young children face the burden of unending jobs on a to-do list, which can become overwhelming. We simply can't fulfill all of our roles—parent, individual, spouse, employee, friend, homemaker and family member—at the same time.

> Ann and Jim have four children (1, 2, 3 and 6 years old) and are struggling with the demands of family, career and community. Ann confides that she is always yelling and, in particular, telling 3-year-old Marta what she's doing wrong—never what she's doing right. Other people at their church think Marta is delightful.
>
> Jim tries to do his best balancing his work schedule, which requires 48-60 hours per week. When he gets home, he suggests to his wife that she take time off and leave the house. But she is so worried that things will fall apart and that the house will be in chaos when she returns that she never goes out without at least two children in tow.
>
> Her mother-in-law, who loves her grandchildren, wonders why Ann and Jim had so many closely spaced children. While she is happy to help on occasion, she believes that her son and daughter-in-law "made their bed."

With deeply held beliefs, even if unrecognized, parents make mundane, yet significant, decisions about many aspects of parenting, including breastfeeding, family bed, potty training, working inside or outside of the home, crying and use of rewards and punishment. Finding one's own voice and perspective on parenting requires pairing child development knowledge with hands-on experience and family and cultural values. Sometimes these overt expectations or surreptitious messages from family, media and cultural norms increase the difficulties of parenting and may put parents or extended family at odds with one another.

Trevon and his family are planning a cross-country trip to their grandparents' home. His son Ian is an active and inquisitive 2-year-old. At home, Ian, the youngest of three, sleeps in a crib. Trevon's father-in-law has made it clear to Trevon and his wife that he does not like the fact that a 2-year-old is still in a crib. He says that when they visit this winter, Ian will sleep in a real bed, not in the portable crib they usually bring with them when they visit.

FROM THE BABY'S POINT OF VIEW

Ian thrives on routines and when things are predictable. When his schedule is disrupted or he misses his nap, it is hard for him to be cooperative, especially at age two. At night, he knows that after he takes a bath, he reads two books on his mom's or dad's lap and then after good night kisses, he goes into his crib. Being in a new environment, especially at night will be a challenge for Ian. He is used to sleeping in his own crib with his special blanket.

"Yesterday I heard myself repeating exactly what
my mom used to say to me and my sister."
Parent

WHAT DO PARENTS NEED?

Being a new parent is sometimes like being a 15-year-old behind the wheel. All those years of observation help, but it's not the same as driving the car. What do parents need to support the healthy development of their baby and their own development as parents?

Parents require know-how and support. In the healthiest of parenting practices, skills and needs are continuously being updated as the child grows and the challenges of parenting change. The U.S. Department of Health and Human Services' Children's Bureau identifies five protective factors linked to healthy outcomes for children and families. Parents who strive to develop these capacities are best equipped to provide the affection, nurturing and discipline necessary to give their children the best chance for developing typically, finding school success, maintaining friendships and developing into competent adults. The five factors are:

- Commitment to nurturing and attachment.
- Knowledge of parenting and child development.
- Parent resilience.
- Social connections.
- Concrete support for parents.

Commitment to nurturing and attachment

Children do well when their parents embrace the critical nature of their jobs in developing the infant's "I matter" attitude and are dedicated to parenting in a responsive, consistent and sensitive manner. Perfect parenting is not the goal. The goal is to understand that the most important part of parenting is a dedication to providing a lasting, secure and trusting relationship in which the parent protects, nurtures and supports the child's developmental success.

Our own experience of being parented, our education/occupation, culture, partner, family and friends shape our understanding of what it means to be a good parent. The correspondence between a parent having developed a secure attachment relationship with her own mother and the quality of the relationship she develops with her baby is about 80 percent. Secure attachment begets secure attachment. Healthy development encourages healthy development.

For some parents, memories and messages may be at odds with the kind of parent they want to be. Their first job is to recognize that past experiences impact current behavior and that we bring forward relationships from our past, particularly our relationships with our own parents. Making a conscious effort about which parenting practices to bring forward and which to leave behind is the next step. Just recognizing what is affecting our relationships is not enough. As adults, we must actively search for models, relationships and strategies that fit with our new standards. Habits learned at a young age are very hard to change, so intentional efforts are essential and can be effective.

Not all adjustments are so easy or ordinary. A parent without a robust appreciation of child development may often misinterpret a child's behavior, such as crying, as an intentional act against the parent. For example, an adult may describe a baby who wants what other babies have as "jealous." Or for a parent to retort, "My baby is trying to make me mad." This can be particularly true when the person became a parent as a teen or was responsible as a young child for the primary care of siblings. In these situations, a parent's ideas about young children are limited by his or her own developmental capacities. Without support, this kind of parent likely will fail to have a more reflective understanding of the infant's behavior.

What about the many well-adjusted adults whose early caregiving experience was punctuated by inconsistent care, neglect, verbal abuse or harsh punishment? Many retrospective studies show that parents who are verbally or physically punitive with their children often were maltreated as children themselves.

Responsive and consistent caregiving can be learned. Parents whose own experiences of being parented were less than stellar must learn to understand themselves and their expectations of relationships through patterns that were developed and reinforced when they were children. Researchers working on the intergenerational cycles of abuse have found that parents who were themselves maltreated but do not harm their children and are able to be emotionally supportive have faced their pasts with honesty and built an emotional awareness of the consequences in their own lives.

Even in the most distorted relationships, in which parents maltreat their young children, 30 percent of those children will become sensitive and responsive parents, breaking the cycle of intergenerational maltreatment. By working to make sense of her early experience from an adult viewpoint, seeing the good with the bad and exploring how these experiences might impact her own role as a parent, she empowers herself to choose what to repeat and what to leave behind. This self-discovery often happens with the help of therapy, parenting groups or important relationships with other adults with secure histories. Researchers refer to this as "earned security" (Sroufe, Egeland, Carlson & Collins, 2005). These individuals have learned to understand themselves through childhood memories and experiences, reconsidering their understanding of their parents' actions. This provides evidence that there are various pathways to competent parenting.

Emily has new insight into her experience as a child of an alcoholic mother. "My mother was not very loving or responsive, but I now understand that she was struggling with alcoholism, was isolated, and had five children under the age of 8. I want to do the very best job at being a mother and I realize that I, too, may make mistakes. Working with a therapist is allowing me to decide what good parts from my relationship with my mother I want to bring forward and what patterns I definitely don't want to repeat. Being a teacher before becoming a mother also helped me develop some behavior management strategies and a more complete understanding of how children develop."

A parent who does not start out with the necessary internal resources can gain greater parenting knowledge, enhance her skills at reading her baby's cues, develop social supports and build adaptive responses to the everyday stresses of parenthood. Parents who find (or learn to find) parenting enjoyable, and who adapt to the experiences brought on by parenthood, tend to provide consistent, nurturing care and have children who are most likely to be successful. Evidence from a study of mothers with a child with an identified disability indicates that a positive attitude towards life, confidence, recognition of strengths and limitations, support and a strong sense of purpose are most likely to create positive outcomes for the child and parent (Gardner & Harmon, 2002).

Whether their commitment is built-in or developed over time, parents must recognize the essential and unique nature of their relationships in the lives of their children. This commitment to nurturance, availability and responsiveness is particularly crucial during the infant and toddler period. Sensitivity and actions that support protecting the quality of the relationship as the parent's central role are the most important contributions. Parent-education programs, home visiting and childcare can reinforce and enhance the essential elements of healthy parent-child relationships and help keep the focus on the parent's central role in protecting and supporting the young child. Simple activities, like saying "goodbye" rather sneaking out of the childcare room at drop-off, reinforce the significance of the relationship.

Knowledge of parenting and child development

Those of us who work with young children often have had the good fortune of learning about child development before becoming parents ourselves. We are naturally curious about how infants and toddlers make sense of their worlds, use two-word sentences, learn to cross midline when drawing with a crayon and climb stairs with alternating feet. It is second nature for us to comment with understanding as a toddler melts down while waiting in a long line. We have already developed a handful of go-to strategies to engage young children in learning and to redirect them when necessary. Gradually, we were able to hone our skills and confidence.

But most parents have not had the same benefit of learning about young children, practicing engagement skills or seeing the benefit of child-oriented interactions with the watchful guidance of professors and without the emotional tugs of parenthood. They are usually building an understanding of development and acquiring skills as their own child grows and develops. Many parents rely on what they experienced as a child or the skills they developed while caring for younger siblings or babysitting. Some read books, ask friends and family or rely on advice from their pediatricians. It does not take a new parent long to recognize that there is a wide range of what is considered typical.

> At age 1, Amanda has a strong preference for her father, who is the parent home with Amanda full-time. In the morning, before bed or when she gets hurt, she only wants her dad. When her mom, Tate, tries to pick her up, Amanda actually screams.

> Tate is feeling as if she is a terrible mother because she works long hours and travels frequently. When Amanda is unhappy, Tate quickly hands her over to her husband. Now Tate is beginning to feel jealous of her husband's relationship with their daughter and questioning her work-family choices.

Having a go-to adult is a sign of healthy and robust development, particularly during the first two years of life. While it feels great to be the go-to-adult and not so great to be "number 2," there are advantages and disadvantages to both. The key is for parents to maintain clear and supportive communication with each other and to remain willing to hear about each other's parenting experiences. The good news is that, babies with parents who worked as partners had greater capacities of self-regulation, fewer behavioral problems and stronger pre-academic skills.

It is easier for parents to negotiate the first year of development when the baby's needs are clear. In infancy, if a parent makes a mistake, for example, changes a diaper when the baby wants to play, the parent can quickly adjust. But toddlerhood seems to sometimes be puzzling for parent and child alike. The terrible twos have become the symbol of development that causes parenting difficulties. Biting, hitting and tantrums, which often emerge at the end of the second year, are usually the parents' first opportunities to decide how to set limits and to help the child learn self-control and pro-social behavior. Most parents need to learn specific techniques to help toddlers and young children handle typical ups and downs, such as not getting a second cookie or leaving a favorite park. Sometimes the toddler doesn't know what he wants and the parent isn't sure how to help him regulate.

Eighteen-month-old Sam has started screaming loudly when his desires are frustrated. He throws himself on the floor and won't stop until he gets what he wants. This became really embarrassing for his mother when Sam threw himself on the floor in the middle of the grocery store. His scream was so disturbing that several people came from other aisles to see what was wrong. His parents don't want to encourage it by giving in to his demands, but they also don't want people to think that they are bad parents who don't know how to discipline their child.

FROM THE BABY'S POINT OF VIEW

Sam experiences life with gusto. He knows what he loves. He knows what he wants. And, when things don't go his way, sometimes the feelings are so big that he has to express them loudly and with his full body. Sometimes the feelings become so big that he forgets what he wanted in the first place.

There are many discipline techniques that can be successful with very young children. Some of the strategies are preemptive, that is, techniques such as distraction or redirection that can be used before a problem behavior emerges. Even a toddler who is ready to bite or hit can be enticed to read a book or sing a song, quickly forgetting the precipitating event that evoked the impulse to lash out. But parents need the opportunities to consider what their limits are and what techniques they want to use. Consistent and reliable limits can also help young children better manage their behaviors. All of us do better when we know the rules, but toddlers, in particular, feel safer when they know someone is helping them set limits.

Parents are most successful when they feel confident and competent in their abilities to adjust their styles and expectations according to the temperament, characteristics and special needs of each of their children. Identifying the special way a baby likes to be held or sleep, a toddler's favorite comfort items or preschooler's favorite foods are often easy, particularly when it is something that relates to the parent's experience.

Some children come with more unique needs, wants and interests—all of which may be typical, but perhaps different from those of their siblings or their parents. When there is a mismatch, perhaps a child who is more sensitive to change, the depth of our child's emotional expression can surprise us. Siblings often take on different roles in the family, which can become more pronounced as they grow. One child might be the resident comedian while another acts as the family's emotional barometer.

> Jada is just recovering from the exhaustion of the feeding, changing diapers, and napping demands of triplet infants. Now at age 2½, her two daughters and son have just started a new preschool. Jada is delighted by the thought of a couple of hours a day of freedom from the limitless demands of parenting.
>
> Jada rejoices that her triplets were born full-term and

have been developmentally on track since birth. However, recently Miranda seems to be extremely sensitive to even the slightest redirection or correction. If Jada asks her to put on her pajamas before she gets a nighttime snack, she cries. After she fights with her siblings and Jada tells her to sit down for a break, she cries and hides her face, refusing to move or look at Jada. When she colors with crayons and doesn't like her picture, Miranda will tear up the paper.

On several occasions, Miranda has told her mom and dad that she doesn't want to go to preschool anymore. Now she's getting weepy when she is at preschool. The teachers report that they are worried because Miranda follows her siblings around and doesn't play with other children. The teachers are recommending that Miranda be transferred to another classroom so she can be more independent of her siblings and learn to play with other children.

Since her other two children seem fine, Jada wonders if this is a typical phase of development or if there is something deeper going on?

A parent is better able to set realistic expectations when she is aware of how development progresses. While parents often understand that a baby will learn to sit up before he will crawl, they often know less about social, emotional and cognitive development. Gaining knowledge about specific stages of development can help prevent misunderstandings about the meaning of a child's behavior.

Daniel attended a special parent-child interaction program at his daughter's childcare center. As part of the parent education section, the adults made play dough, which they later brought into the childcare room to share with their toddlers. The parent educator prepared the parents for what they might expect when they entered the room and began playing with their children and the play dough. She helped them practice a few handy strategies to create a warm parent-child interaction using the play dough. She also forecast that a few toddlers might want to taste the play dough, and suggested a quick response of "no mouth" would help the play materials from becoming a slimy mess. She reminded parents that we use short and direct statements because toddlers tend to only remember the last two words said.

The teacher noticed that Daniel, sitting at the table with his daughter, Makayla, looked tense when Makayla started to move the play dough towards her mouth.

"Stop putting the play dough in your mouth!" Makayla startled at the sound of her dad's voice, then again began moving her hand towards her mouth.

Daniel looked at the parent educator. "Oh, yeah," he said, and then turned to his daughter. "No mouth," he said as he reached over and gently stopped his daughter's arm before it reached her mouth.

Informal and formal playgroups, talking with childcare providers and parent education classes can facilitate these conversations and opportunities for parents to update their understanding of child development as their children progress and they encounter new joys and challenges.

Parent resilience

Parenthood brings with it intensely demanding tasks and interactions. It is a job in which problems are expected and anticipated. The sheer exhaustion produced by sleep deprivation and the constant need to be "on" requires internal fortitude, flexibility and external support. Resilience is the ability to adapt to this ever-changing landscape of needs and requirements, interactions and distractions within the mundane monotony of everyday meals, diapers and laundry. For most parents, the motto, "The days are long but the years are short," rings true.

Parenthood is a 24/7 job. And with children under the age of 5, it is one of the world's most emotionally and physically exhausting positions. We simply can't fulfill all of our roles—parent, individual, spouse, employee, friend, homemaker and family member—at the same time. It's always a trade-off and almost all parents feel or want to do more.

> "Why did I have such mixed feelings on Mother's Day? I love my children. My husband helped them make me cute cards and we went out to breakfast to celebrate. But I still had to keep the baby entertained during breakfast, do the laundry when we got home and go to the grocery store. What I really wanted for Mother's Day was to get the day off! Then I felt terrible about having these thoughts."

It's perfectly reasonable, and relatively common, that a mother's wish for Mother's Day was to get a break from the mundane responsibilities of parenting. Parents need to realize that it is okay and healthy to ask for what you need and to model self-care by seeking support. Sometimes parents hear a message that says "a good mother shouldn't feel _____ (fill in the blank) or need _____."

We learn to manage everyday and extraordinary stress through past experiences, our own internal resources, family expectations and cultural values. Even positioning Mother's Day as stressful may cross the line of acceptability. But our abilities to openly recognize stress and then regulate our own daily experiences builds resiliency. Our awareness and strengths guide us towards our coping strategies. Using humor, talking with supportive individuals, creative problem-solving, striving to be flexible and leaning on community culture and faith all help build self-awareness and the capacity to cope.

As anyone knows who has found themselves staring into the refrigerator without being hungry, kicked the dog or drunk alcohol from a coffee mug first thing in the morning, we have methods for managing stress that are not always good for us. Adults have to understand and implement their own healthy approaches for balance and renewal. Parents need a toolbox of effective stress-management strategies.

Parents need to understand the impact of stress on their children and to develop strategies to protect their children from the full impact of adversity. Our resiliency and stress management techniques give our children a model for dealing effectively with life's ups and downs. Using typical situations to model coping strategies can assist children in learning to regulate their own emotional arousal to stress and responses to unpredictable situations.

FROM THE BABY'S POINT OF VIEW

When Dad spills the milk and says, "Accidents happen, even to dads," it helps Jenee build confidence that she, too, can manage the inevitable mishaps of daily life.

Parents who have flexibility and inner strength can manage the unexpected or chronic events themselves, as well as buffer their children. When parents engage in short-term supports, such as getting help from grandparents during an unexpected illness, and model effective coping strategies, they give their children confidence that there will always be adults to care for them.

If a child feels unprotected, he must begin anticipating threatening situations at a young age; he begins to worry about problems that are more complex than he is able to solve. This heightened worry makes him unable to maintain attention, manage his emotions and engage in learning. In the best interest of every child, the exposure to adverse events must be contained. This is particularly true for young children living in neighborhoods or in families in which acts of violence and illicit activities are more prevalent. The more stressful life events experienced by the child, the more likely that his brain will adapt to the constant presence of threat and harm.

Parents need the opportunity to evaluate their ways of coping with stress to determine if those used in the past are effective in parenthood. Self-help books, parenting groups and other forms of informal and formal support groups through the neighborhood, school district or religious community can offer parents ideas and reinforce self-care and strong problem-solving skills. Activities such as deep breathing, exercise, socializing and even daily routines can enhance feelings of wellness and competence during periods of calm and provide a source of comfort during stress. Many parents may find solace in spiritual or religious practices, counseling, education or social support groups. The key is to integrate stress-management techniques into the busy lives of parents with the higher purpose of being a better parent.

Social connections

Having a co-parent to share the work, solve problems and provide emotional support and economic security will strengthen child outcomes. In terms of healthy child development, it doesn't matter if this partnership is a marriage or a permanent living arrangement. What does matter is that the co-parenting relationship is characterized by low conflict, good communication and joint decision-making. These factors engender the security, responsiveness and consistency needed for secure parent-child attachment. Social support from parent to parent can also mediate the quality and continuity of the attachment relationship with the child. Date nights, common interests and shared appreciation can help relationships weather the demands of parenthood.

Strong ties and involvement with extended family can also serve as a protective factor and have a positive impact on young children. Special attachments with other adults can increase the abilities of children to manage challenging life circumstances (Werner, 1999).

Typically, these relationships are characterized by the adult's ability to engage in a caring and consistent relationship with the child, maintain high expectations for success and provide opportunities for the child and adult to participate and contribute together to the overall health of the family, school or community. Relationships with other caring adults can buffer young children from the impact of stressful life events by nurturing their abilities to make use of or to benefit from protective opportunities and building empathy and concern for others.

In the Family Assets study conducted by the Search Institute, a national not-for-profit organization, researchers found that the greatest needs for American families were in the areas of "establishing routines," "adapting to challenges" and "connecting to community" (Syvertsen et al, 2012). The type of parenting that is effective also may be dependent on the families' and neighborhood's resources. For example, children who grow up in neighborhoods of high poverty and violence do better when firm rules and control over the child's whereabouts are present, unlike parenting in lower-risk environments, where flexibility has greater benefits (Titterton, Hill & Smith, 2002; Syvertsen et al, 2011).

Most parent-focused programs also provide structured and unstructured education and support groups. Parent-child parenting classes and unstructured playgroups are a great way to learn and practice at the same time. Parents see close-up the wide variations in typical development, get a peek into the next stage of development, ask questions of other parents with similar experiences—and have a good laugh. Most parents need the opportunity to learn teaching techniques, such as limit-setting, redirecting behaviors and settling routines. These learning opportunities allow parents to build realistic expectations of their own children's behavior and to develop sturdy communication skills to express high expectations with warmth and understanding.

It tends to be most helpful when parenting groups have time built in to explore opinions, share personal experiences and summarize research-based advice. For many parents, it helps to know that "we're all in this together." Social connections built through membership in a faith community or cultural practice can be protective by providing social and spiritual support (Werner, 1990; Syvertsen et al, 2011). Multiple and varied opportunities for social engagement, parent education and parent-child interactions work best under these conditions.

School-based early education parenting and parent-child groups promote positive parenting skills and support. These programs can build early and positive relationships between school district personnel and parents, as well as family-to-family connections. Typically, these groups are weekly, age-based opportunities that provide time for parent exchanges and discussion of development, as well as for structured parent-child interactions. Early Head Start and Head Start provide these same kinds of opportunities through Health Families and other such programs. These programs are most successful when parents are highly motivated to connect with others and to build knowledge or when the program is very intentional about inviting families, creates welcoming and engaging formats and designs appealing and valued programs that can rival the other demands on the family's time.

Concrete support

Many parent-support and home-visiting programs focus initially on establishing social connections and concrete support for basic needs as methods of building connections with parents and ensuring child well-being. There is strong evidence that these protective factors are important. While poverty or affluence is not an independent risk factor in parenting, variables such as social connectedness, violence and safe environments can enhance or stymie parents' abilities to be emotionally protective and supportive. Neighborhoods, particularly Socioeconomic Status (SES), do impact child outcomes (Brooks-Gunn & Markman, 2005; Leventhal & Brooks-Gunn, 2002). A recent study of infants born during periods of high unemployment found a significant increase in the likelihood of delinquent behaviors and substance abuse as teenagers (Ramanathan, Balasubramania & Krishnadas, 2012).

Families that lack sufficient food, secure shelter and a safe environment must expend significant resources on these basic needs, leaving less time and energy for engaging with children. Even when community resources are available in the form of utility vouchers, furniture, food and housing, many families are either unaware of such services or conflicted about using them. Financial stressors such as unemployment, job transitions and housing foreclosure can limit a parent's capacity to nurture and support her children. Women and single heads of households are most vulnerable to financial stress; the report documents that women are three times more likely than men to face "overwhelming financial stress." For parents employed outside of the home, quality childcare that is affordable is essential. Many families spend 10 percent of their paycheck on childcare.

Numerous studies document direct links between financial stress and physical and mental health problems. Health issues combined with stress predictably make parenting more difficult and increase the vulnerability of the parent-child relationship. For women, financial difficulties are most related to psychological problems such as anxiety and increased rates of smoking (which in turn have significant negative impact on birth outcomes).

Many prevention and intervention programs focus on providing or linking families with job training, childcare, health care and housing, while providing winter coats, diapers, car seats and other basics. In the effort to supply basic needs and help families connect with resources, providers whose focus is on improving parenting outcomes may soon tire of being a taxi service. Often in case consultation, a home visitor or public health nurse will question why parents always ask for necessities or rides, failing to realize that provision of these items and services was the first "contract" they made with the family.

When families, neighborhoods and communities come together to support our children, we raise them to be caring, contributing adults. We could make significant gains in ensuring the healthy development of children if we found ways to integrate opportunities and supports into our neighborhoods and communities, in order to engage all families with young children. Remember that imbedded in the definition of mental health supplied by Parlakian & Seibel (2002) is the "context of family, community and cultural expectations for young children."

Secure attachment between baby and parent becomes the prototype for later relationships. It's fortified by successful relationships with teachers and peers and, eventually, romantic relationships. The child develops a working model for going out into the world and managing daily ups and downs. These models are relatively stable, operating across the child's lifespan—including when she becomes a parent herself.

"She was acting naughty so I took her beloved blanket
away and she proceeded to get MAD."
Parent

IS THERE A PARENTING PROBLEM?

Insecure Attachment

Babies are "hard-wired" to expect comfort and interactions with their primary caregivers. And, a child's basic foundation allows for her parents—mere mortals, after all—to make occasional mistakes. A parent rarely gets everything right. But if the child's typical experience is of consistent and nurturing care, her foundation will be solid. A child cries for her mother because she wants a response. Through their interactions with primary caregivers, babies learn what to expect the next time.

But, even when a parent is trying hard to provide a secure foundation for her child, internal and external factors may inhibit the consistency or predictability of the parent's responses. The interactive pattern between baby and parent may be disrupted, causing one or both partners to become unpredictable or difficult to satisfy. Both baby and parent bring things to their relationship that can be potential triggers for disrupting the consistency, enjoyment or satisfaction.

After enlisting the help of an infertility specialist with her first pregnancy, Megan and her husband were overjoyed when they became pregnant with their second child. While getting pregnant was much easier, Megan began to worry about how she would managing working 30 hours a week while overseeing her household and a very active 2-year-old. The second pregnancy was also physically more challenging. Megan experienced significant morning sickness and during her seventh month of pregnancy was hospitalized for two weeks with hyperemesis.

Following the birth of her second daughter, Cara, Megan described the birth as "an ordeal." It was nothing like her first baby, who was born by caesarean section; Megan felt that Cara "made a mess" of her. Because of the medical complications, Megan was not able to hold Cara right away. While she regretted that she missed that moment to bond with her newborn, she felt that Cara wasn't a very cuddly baby anyway.

Cara was a persistent crier, often described as colicky. Although exhausted, Megan was eager to return to work after her six-week maternity leave to get a break from Cara's crying. The beloved home-based childcare provider she used for her older daughter was unable to provide care for the infant, so Megan enrolled both daughters in a childcare center close to her work. She dropped the girls off at the center at 7 am before their regular teachers arrived so that she could pick them up by 3 pm. Her older daughter's eyes filled with tears as soon as they pulled into the parking lot. Once they were inside the center, the teacher would try to distract Megan's older daughter so Megan could leave quickly.

Megan found herself resenting Cara's arrival in their family. Her crying, the resulting change in childcare providers and the demands of taking care of two children felt overwhelming. At night, Megan dreaded getting up to feed Cara and at times, would just let her cry herself to sleep or wait for her husband to respond to Cara's needs. The joy she experienced in caring for her older child seamed to evaporate when it came to caring for Cara. While feeling guilty about these disparate feelings, she didn't know how to change them.

While colic can subside, a difficult pregnancy and early parenting woes can influence the way a parent thinks about and responds to her baby. Repeated experiences mold the way in which baby learns about her own power, and place in the world. Her bids for reassurance result in an accumulated history of failure in her attempts to have her needs met and her emotional expressions understood. Over time, when faced with unpredictable or unresponsive reactions from her parent, the baby learns to rely on behaviors like clinging and whining to manage her own distress at the parent's inconsistencies.

> During a walk around the neighborhood, Megan confides to her friend Patty that, while she adores her 3-year-old daughter, she dreads each minute she has to spend with her 18-month-old daughter. "From the moment Cara wakes up, she is constantly calling for me. She won't let me out of her sight. If I need to take a basket of laundry to the basement, she clings to my leg. I am left with the option of trying to get down the stairs with the basket and Cara in tow, or leaving her at the top of the stairs wailing until I return. During these times I just want to get away from her. It is like this all of the time. No matter where I go, she has to follow me. When I sit down with her in our family room, she won't play by herself. And if I play with her, she often throws toys or tries to hurt me."

FROM THE BABY'S POINT OF VIEW

Cara desperately wants her mother's attention and love. And some times she gets it. But other times, Cara's mom doesn't respond when she calls out for help or names a animal that she sees out of the window of the car. Sometimes her mother watches television or plays with Cara's sister but doesn't seem to notice Cara. So Cara gets in the middle of the game they are playing or makes a big fuss. Not knowing when her mother will be loving and when she will ignore her, Cara watches her mom closely. She follows her wherever she goes and becomes inconsolable when separated, even when it is only for a few minutes. When together, Cara spends most of her time thinking about her mom and when she might leave or be disapproving. Playing, being with friends or discovering new things are much less important than making sure her mom is within arm's reach. She constantly searches for security in this essential relationship.

It's a push-me-pull-you scenario in which parent and child can't get it right often enough to form a harmonious attachment relationship. While the child is depending on her mother for comfort, reassurance and regulation, she is also an active participant and contributor to the type of response she receives. Cara's clinging, whining, and lack of fulfillment increase the likelihood of inconsistent, insensitive responses. It is hard to care for a child who just "can't get enough."

Researchers call the type of relationship shared by Megan and Cara an insecure attachment. As a result of the instability, insensitivity or lack of responsiveness of the parent's affection and attention, the toddler develops strategies. For toddlers, like Cara, whose primary relationship with her mother has been rejection of her pleas for attention and regulation, shutting down, avoiding contact and expectations and limiting emotional expressions are typical.

Toddlers similar to Cara respond to the reunification scenario of the Ainsworth Strange Situation by becoming demanding and switching between wanting to be held and then placed on the floor in a pattern of engaging and disengaging. These inconsistent interactions increase anxiety in both mother and child, threatening the ability of each to elicit the desired response from the other.

A mother who has developed an anxious attachment relationship with her child experiences more anxiety and stress in her parenting role than mothers with secure attachment relationships. Megan's pattern of interaction with her baby is likely a response to unpredictable care during the first several months of life. Megan's postpartum depression eroded her desire and ability to meet Cara's needs for interaction and comfort. Cara responded by intensifying her emotional responses and learned that her mom is not a reliable regulatory partner.

Children with insecure attachments with their primary caregivers tend to be less emotionally reactive at age 14 months but, by 33 months, they are highly reactive and showing significantly more negative emotions, even in situations that are experienced by securely attached preschool-age children as joyful (Sroufe, Egeland, Carlson, & Collins, 2005). A child with an insecure parent-child attachment relationship is more likely to be the socially immature preschooler who hovers near teachers and looks for nurturing instead of playing with friends. The lack of confidence in caregiver availability compromises her ability to learn and build peer relationships. In elementary school, these same children behave as if they're anticipating rejection by their peers, making it easy for other children to do just that.

Insecure attachment relationships produce in children strategic behavior patterns of managing anxiety while striving to connect securely. A child cries for her mother because she wants a response. But she protects herself by rebuffing her mother's attempts, even when her mother is making an effort. Babies continually revise and update their perceptions of how relationships work based on the reinforcement they get (or don't get) from their parents. Security in primary relationships is the ultimate goal.

The good news is that responsive and consistent caregiving can be learned. A parent who does not start out with the necessary internal resources can develop adaptive responses to stressful circumstances, enhanced interpersonal skills, and a greater base of parenting knowledge.

Attachment

Normal development is resilient but not unbreakable. Babies who witness trauma will predictably feel unsafe and apprehensive. If a parent's behaviors consistently alarm rather than reassure the child, the result is the most clinically worrisome attachment relationship: disorganized/disoriented attachment. If the cornerstone of a secure attachment relationship is the child's perception that the parent can protect her, early maltreatment causes a child biologically wired to seek comfort to do so knowing that she may be harmed. This prevents her from developing a coherent strategy for signaling her needs.

Three year-old Madison sits at the kitchen table coloring while her 7-month-old sister, Jasmine, who is buckled into her stroller, sits next to her. Jasmine arches her back trying to get out of the stroller, grunts and then settles back into the stroller. Their mother, Joslyn, ignores both children as she places a pan of pizza rolls into the oven. A barking neighbor dog causes Jasmine to startle and fuss. Joslyn ignores her. Jasmine attempts to calm herself; she looks at her hands, sucks on her fingers, and begins to hiccup. Another loud bark causes Jasmine to furrow her brow and fuss again, with more agitation.

Joslyn's voice is quick and harsh: "Stop fussing. You're not the only one in the house who wants to eat."

Jasmine briefly stops fussing but is now unable to manage her worry alone. She lets out a loud wail. Her mom pulls her out of her seat, grabs a bottle and sits down to feed her.

Joslyn tells Jasmine, "You can't always get what you want; the world ain't like that."

As she feeds Jasmine, Joslyn thinks about the fight she just had with Jasmine's father, which ended with him leaving to drink beer with his buddies while she got stuck taking care of their two children. Joslyn's foot starts to swing and her jaw clenches. Jasmine senses the change in her mom's demeanor and stops drinking to look up at her.

Joslyn responds, "You don't want to eat? Fine, the rest of us do." She takes Jasmine to the bedroom, deposits her in her crib, and walks out, shutting the door behind her. Joslyn turns on the radio to drown out the wails of her infant daughter.

FROM THE BABY'S POINT OF VIEW

With no cognitive ability to take the perspective of others, Jasmine only understands her experience. She does not know about the fight or mom's feelings. She only feels the tension and knows that something is different. When these unpredictable and severe consequences occur, Jasmine's limited abilities conclude that her bids for attention sometimes result in positive ways and sometime result in harm or abandonment.

Jasmine's response to her mom's tension reminds us that very young babies are more keenly aware of sights, sounds and sensations, and easily detect changes in a caregiver's body language and facial expressions. Parents used to be told that babies don't have the capacity to notice or feel small changes in the environment. We know now that this is not true.

Disorganized/disoriented attachment results from parent

behaviors that may initially seem loving but often become intrusive or frightening (Carlson, 1998). A parent who once or twice embraces her child while gritting her teeth and scolding her is having a bad day. A parent who does this often, sends her child conflicting emotional messages. Mental illness and domestic abuse situations can produce the same effect: A usually competent caregiver becomes emotionally or physically unable to care for or protect her child.

A child who experiences both loving and frightening interactions with the same parent, over time develops a repertoire of ineffective, poorly organized and atypical behaviors such as clinginess, aggression, fear and confusion. He accumulates a series of failures in gaining appropriate attention coupled with repeated experiences of helplessness, harm and alarm. Researchers observe that such a child will often hold his arms up to a parent to be held while at the same time turning his head away with a worried or frightened look.

Within a disorganized attachment relationship, the child behaves erratically because he believes that there is no real connection between asking for what he wants or needs and getting it. A baby is by nature egocentric, believing that their behaviors are what control the world. For a baby in a disorganized relationship, she never knows if it will be the "good" or the "hurting" mommy. We believe that because of the limited cognitive capacities of the baby, the baby has difficulty building successful emotional capacities for regulation, relationships and communication.

In a meta-analysis of 80 attachment studies, researchers determined that in low-risk samples, about 15 percent of parent-infant relationships develop disorganized attachments. When an infant or toddler has experienced maltreatment or neglect, nearly half of the parent-infant relationships demonstrate disorganized patterns of interaction.

Without significant intervention, children whose early intimate relationships are disorganized by maltreatment and/or neglect have little confidence that they will be successful in other relationships, challenges or endeavors. By age 6, they are more aggressive towards peers, demonstrate more behavioral problems and display poorer impulse control than securely attached children (Sroufe, Egeland, Carlson & Collins, 2005).

These negative behaviors set up a kind of self-perpetuating cycle, reinforcing to themselves and others that they are not capable of being nurtured and loved. By adolescence, they express emotional and personality disturbances as a result of disordered self-organization and limited abilities to think about behaviors more than "good" and "bad." Borderline Personality Disorder, which is characterized by a longing for intimacy coupled with overwhelming concern about being rejected, is theorized to be related to disorganized attachment relationships (Fonagy, Target & Gergely, 2000). In a review of 13 clinical studies, strong evidence was found to support the development of Borderline Personality Disorder (Agrawal, Gunderson, Holmes, & Lyons-Ruth, 2004).

Neurobiology of Relationships

A growing body of research suggests that early experiences become biologically embedded. That is, quality attachment relationships not only support physical and emotional development but also influence a child's neurological development. Brains control behavior therefore children's behavioral development is an expression of their brain development. By the end of a child's first year, this attachment pattern has begun to influence how a child responds to stress physiologically. Through the development of noninvasive methods of measuring cortisol—a hormone central to the flight-or-fight reactions in humans—researchers are now able to assess this response.

The research of Megan Gunnar and colleagues reveals that the quality of an attachment relationship does indeed correspond to the child's physiological reaction to stress (Gunnar, Bodersen, Nachmais, Buss, & Rigatuso, 1996; Gunnar, Herrera, Hostinar, 2009). One study examined children's behavioral and physiological responses to inoculations during each of their well-child medical visits at ages 2, 4, 6 and 18 months. (At 15 months, researchers measured the security of their attachment relationships using Mary Ainsworth's Strange Situation tool.)

Not surprisingly, most of the babies cried when they got their shots (one in each thigh). As they got older, however, many showed smaller and smaller cortisol responses until at 18 months they showed no increase at all, even while getting their booster shots. Not all followed this pattern; some continued to show spikes in cortisol levels when receiving their shots. The analysis revealed that the children in secure relationships were the ones whose stress levels dropped over time simply by virtue of having their responsive caregiver in the room. The amounts of cortisol measured in children with insecure attachments who had their caregiver with them, conversely, continued to elevate as they became older.

While the reactions of the children looked similar (distressed, worried or unhappy), their physiological reactions to stress differed significantly. Young children with secure attachment relationships counted on their caregiver to help them manage stress. In contrast, infants with an insecure pattern of attachment engaged a hormonal response (cortisol) to the perceived threat. They knew not to count on their adult caregiver for comfort. Occasional increases in cortisol levels are normal. Sustained and elevated amounts of cortisol, however, can have long-term effects, making children vulnerable to memory loss, impaired learning and a decrease in the body's ability to heal itself (Rutter et al, 2010).

In another study, researchers presented 18-month-old children with a clown, a strange puppet and a noisy mechanical toy. As expected, about half of the children found these things a bit scary; regardless of their attachment history they showed wariness and behaviors indicating that these things worried them. Interestingly, some of these wary responders showed no cortisol response while others showed large increases. Again, the difference between the children's physiological stress levels was not the degree of stress but the security of their attachment relationships. Fearful children in secure relationships showed no increase in their level of stress hormone. Fearful children in insecure relationships showed significant increases.

By their second year of life, children have logged thousands of everyday moments during feeding, changing, bath and playtime that tell them about their ability to enlist the help of adults in managing novel or traumatic experiences. Physiologically, this history dictates whether young children come to believe that, in any given situation, they can count on the adults in their lives to help them manage perceived challenges or whether they must count more on their own immature hormonal reactions to protect themselves.

Under extreme conditions, the fight-or-flight response works for adults. A very young child who is unable to understand the risk or to stand up to the modern equivalent of a saber-tooth tiger, however, simply becomes overwhelmed by biological reactions, including an inflammatory reaction (most notably involving C-reactive proteins, which prepare for a quick response to a physical injury). When the attack is psychological, however, the C-reactive proteins circulate at a higher than normal rate without a physical injury to heal. A growing body of research suggests that repeat exposures to childhood toxic stress—especially in the absence of a protective adult—increases the likelihood of a child later developing inflammatory disease, including diabetes, heart disease and early mortality (Shonkoff et al, 2012).

We also know that repeated exposure to stressful life events lowers the threshold at which the stress response system kicks in. Our biological systems are designed to handle periodic extreme stress. But with repeated exposure to toxic stress, the body begins to perceive even modest threats as acutely dangerous. A child who has experienced maltreatment or chronic neglect may experience a challenging math problem as stressful or scary and react out of proportion to a situation the teacher perceives as no big deal.

By the Numbers

Although cases of insecure parent-child relationships should be rare, they are all too prevalent. Using the Ainsworth Attachment Classification system, a recent national study of more than 100 children from various regions of the United States confirmed that only

60 percent of parents and young children in the general population form secure attachments (NICHD Research Network, 2006). Most alarmingly, almost half of the remaining 40 percent of the parent-child relationships were determined to be disorganized. We have an emotional readiness gap of 35 percent that is measurable as early as 18 months of age. Baby's brains are vulnerable to toxic environments and interactions, but they are also remarkably flexible and responsive to interventions that aim to restore—within safe and responsive environments—the child's sense of security in his relationships.

5

"We cannot ask infants what they mean but can only infer meaning from the infants' behavior."
Ed Tronick, PhD

DISRUPTERS IN READINESS

The idiom, "The baby has a face only a mother could love," speaks to our societal belief of the unconditional adoration and the diving force of a mother's ability to focus on the inner beauty of her child. What happens when a parent doesn't feel instantaneous and overwhelming love for her child or when physical or behavior difficulties impact a parent's approach or connection? While many parents can manage these initial reactions and adjustments to the unexpected outcome of the child's birth or challenging characteristics, for some, the challenges their child brings into the relationship may be more than they expected. These unexpected, conflicting emotions in parenthood are widely experienced but almost taboo to discuss in most playgroups, coffee klatches and family gatherings—yet they can have a significant impact on the developing parent-child relationship.

Changes in the availability, consistency and presence of the primary caregiver can also significantly impact a child's development and sense of security in the parent-child relationship. Depending on the child's age and stage of development, separations can rock even secure attachments and disrupt the child's sense of confidence and building of trusting relationships. Some separations—intended or unintended, physical or psychological—can have negative impact on the parent-child relationship and the child's sense of confidence and may significantly alter emotional development. Vacations, hospitalizations, military deployment, depression, divorce and foster placement are all examples of life circumstances that profoundly change the availability of primary caregivers. A baby can experience grief and loss upon significant separation from her known primary caregivers, whether the separation is for a few weeks or permanently.

"There was absolutely nothing we could
do to soothe her. Nothing."
Grandparent

CHILD-RELATED DISRUPTERS

The U.S. Department of Health and Human Services Children's Bureau recently added a sixth protective factor linked to healthy outcomes for children and families: Social Emotional Competence of the Child. As any parent knows from dealing with a tantrum in the parking lot or at a family gathering, there are moments when our resolve is tested. Even more broadly, parenting, educating and nurturing is much easier when a child's development is typical and when she has the ability to make friends, manage her feelings and be excited by learning. When a child's cues and signals are clear and easily answered, parenting is rewarding. It is easier for parents to understand when a child is excited, sad, loving or frustrated when the child's behavior directly matches her experiences. A child who cries frequently, is over-reactive to touch or who is preoccupied by worries makes it more difficult for the parents to be consistent with strategies, manage the child's and her own frustrations and find joy in countless and mundane everyday moments.

We are not used to thinking that a baby can add anything but joy to the parent-child relationship, which means we attribute problems to parents and make interventions with them, rather than with babies. For example, when a young mother complains that her 4-month-old doesn't like to be held, a home visitor is likely to intervene by examining the mother's approach to holding the baby, rather than looking at the baby's reaction to being held. The child who resists wearing scratchy clothes may have first protested snuggling as an infant because of a physiological heightened sensitivity to touch. When a baby doesn't like to be held and her mother and others blame the mother's behavior, it can cause rejection and frustration in the relationship.

The baby's growing ability to communicate her needs and desires makes social interactions more enjoyable for baby and caregiver alike, ultimately developing the important relationship skills necessary for emotional health. However, sometimes the baby brings risks and resiliencies into the developing relationship with his parents. Even when a parent is trying hard to provide a secure foundation for her child and to respond consistently to her baby's cues, other factors may inhibit her responses.

While many parents are able to navigate a divergent course with great dexterity, developmental disability makes it more difficult for the parent to accurately read and feel competent in responding to the child's cues and signals. For example, activities that normally would elicit a bright smile and engaging cooing, when attempted with a child with sensory integration difficulties, may leaving a parent feeling unrewarded and rejected.

Children with biological challenges (e.g. cognitive delays, prematurity, sensory integration difficulties) are at risk for developing insecure attachment relationships. For example, a baby who is averse to being touched may push away from his mother as she attempts to cuddle him or may avoid making eye contact with her as she tries to tickle his belly. Without support and guidance, these early relationships can get off track, significantly impacting parents' sense of confidence and connectedness to their babies and a baby's developmental trajectory. Children with biological challenges (e.g. cognitive delays, pre-maturity, sensory integration difficulties) are at risk for developing insecure attachment relationships (Cassidy & Shaver, 2008).

All children have strengths and vulnerabilities. Many of us have seen in our own children that one size does not fit all. Some kids are just "higher maintenance." In other words, "good enough" parenting for one child may not be quite good enough for another. Children and adults bring vulnerabilities to their relationships and to the tasks before them. What are the conditions that result in a more difficult to care for baby or a child who has more challenges with engaging in relationships, regulating emotion and learning?

Prematurity and Medical Complications

Thanks to huge advances in medicine, babies who wouldn't have survived at other times in history are able to thrive today with a variety of short- and long-term medical interventions. It is easy to understand why parents of a premature infant would be stressed and anxious. Premature babies may face serious medical conditions, long stays in the NICU and unpredictable feeding, wake and sleep cycles (Browne, 2003).

Many parents of premature babies are surprised and guilt-ridden by their initial responses to the newborn. Having expected to feel overwhelming feelings of joy and love, parents of extremely small babies may not immediately feel bonded and connected, may be disheartened by the size and shape of their baby and may protect themselves by separating from the infant or, alternately, incessantly hovering over the isolette. In the NICU, "unusual" parenting behaviors may be enhanced if the staff inadvertently convey messages of maternal fault or inadequacies or accuse (overtly or subtly) the parent of neglecting the newborn through infrequent visitation.

By understanding the effects of these conditions on the parent, we can more easily identify the strategies that will help the parent respond sensitively to the baby's cues and signals and respond in ways that help the child better organize and gain confidence in himself and others.

When prematurity or a medical or developmental condition changes the course of the milestone pathway, naturally occurring moments of delight are obscured. Many parents are able to navigate this divergent course with great dexterity, but developmental disabilities do make it more difficult for parents to accurately read and feel competent in responding to a child's cues and signals. Without support, a baby who has poor oral skills and who takes an hour to feed can leave parents with overwhelming feelings of burden and despair.

Persistent Crying

Babies differ in how, when and how long they cry. Some babies only fuss after waiting a long time for what they need; others begin to wail at the first twinge of distress. The cries of newborns are meant to signal an alarm: "Pay attention to me now!" Given the helplessness of newborns, this demanding cry is designed to get immediate adult attention. Babies benefit from adult responses—soothing, rocking, singing and cuddling, which begin to develop emotional regulation and establish the attachment relationship.

When this high-pitched alarm cry is persistent and excessive, it may be called colic. Babies who are colicky are persistent criers who react more quickly with a cry than other babies during their first few months of life. Persistent and frequent criers demonstrate difficulties in arousal and calming. Carrying a baby who cries persistently can help reduce the duration of the crying (calming) but not the frequency (arousal). It appears that holding infants helps them regulate the intensity of their reactions, letting them learn early to use a parent as a partner in regulating emotional experiences.

> "My baby is 6 weeks old and cries constantly. The only time she stops crying is when I hold her. I am exhausted and really wondering if I will be a good mother to her. My other children never cried like this."

Persistent crying usually peaks at about 6 weeks, but the impact on the parent-child relationship can linger. Excessive crying is not an indicator of a child with a difficult temperament, but parents tend to see their previously "colicky" babies as having more difficult natures. Nevertheless, researchers have found no differences in behavior between toddlers who were once persistent criers and those who were not.

Regulatory Difficulties

Many of us have fond memories of rocking our infants to sleep or introducing them to a new flavor of baby food. These everyday moments provide a sense of accomplishment and connection and reflect the importance of establishing basic biological patterns in the first year of life for healthy development. But when a toddler never sleeps through the night or an infant takes two hours to feed, these natural parenting joys can be tarnished. Tantrums at the table, refusal to use the potty or sleep issues can test the resolve and quality of attachment relationships. In these situations, the balance of control can slip into the child's corner, chipping away at the stability of the relationship.

An immature regulation system can interfere with a baby's abilities to perceive and accept comfort and emotional responsiveness from others. Unfortunately for both child and parent, this can become a cycle of poor regulation, misinterpretation and misalignment of signals and responses, increasing the likelihood of insecure attachment behaviors. Babies may also have difficulty establishing regular sleep and eating patterns, further exacerbating parents' sense of incompetence and lack of internal resources. Crying, sleeping and eating deregulation can trigger a cycle within the child's internal system, causing significant parent distress. This, in turn, is may be physically and verbally transferred back to the child, creating a cycle of distress and dissatisfaction. Babies who are particularly irritable in stressful situations are somewhat more likely to develop insecure attachments with their primary caregivers. These difficulties in regulation likely require "extras" from the parent in order to respond consistently and sensitively.

FROM THE BABY'S POINT OF VIEW

If she were older and had the words, 4-month-old Jenny would tell her mom that the tag on the back of her shirt feels like pins sticking into her neck. If she were older, she might be able to say that when she arches her back while being held, it is because having her body touch someone else's is unbearable.

Feeding problems, particularly picky eating, overeating or refusing food altogether, can occur within relationships that are secure and responsive, but it's easy to see how feeding difficulties can diminish the joys of child-parent interactions and escalate into power struggles and fits of frustration for parent and child alike. The increased conflict can result in an insecure attachment relationship, which then compounds the feeding problems and potentially can lead to malnutrition.

Like consistent and healthy feeding patterns, consistent sleep patterns and regular sleep and waking periods, known as circadian rhythms, are an essential component of early development. Keeping a regular sleep schedule helps train babies' brains and bodies to sleep when it's dark and be awake when it's light. A chaotic sleep pattern, when a baby naps more during the day, is difficult to get to sleep at night and/or wakes frequently, begins a cycle of sleep deprivation for baby and parents. As the parent of a child who was diagnosed and treated for sleep apnea at age 2, I can attest to the challenges of finding the right diagnosis, the impact of sleep deprivation and the failure of multiple strategies designed to "train" a child to sleep.

Alcohol and Drug Exposure

An estimated 14 percent of women use alcohol or binge drink during pregnancy (Ethen et al, 2009). The effects of prenatal alcohol exposure are widely known, but they can vary significantly among children and may go undetected during the first few years of development. Even if the alcohol exposure and the extent of the neural damage remain undiscovered, the impact on both the child's development and the parent-child relationship are substantial.

Fetal Alcohol Syndrome effects for older children are well documented, but the more subtle effects during the infant and toddler period may be overlooked, misinterpreted or dismissed. An infant's difficulties with eating, sleeping, irritability and other physiological interactions may be a result of prenatal alcohol exposure. These undetected neurological difficulties can significantly interfere with the success of attachment relationships. A baby may be very irritable and difficult to soothe, leaving a parent with the feeling that nothing he or she does makes the baby happy. Because prenatal alcohol exposure can influence sensory development, a baby may be especially reactive to loud noises and bright lights or—most devastating to a relationship—sensitive to touch.

"When a parent is too-much missed, too-long absent, the child is overcome by yearning and sadness. Images, feelings and memories usually so assuring provoke, increasingly, unhappiness and despair."

Jeere Pawl, PhD

PARENT-CHILD RELATIONSHIP DISRUPTERS

Separation

Awareness of separation from primary caregivers begins to emerge at about 6 months of age. At the same time, the child's abilities to express preference for being close to and wanting the presence of her parents becomes increasingly apparent. When dad walks out of the room, the baby crawls to follow him. If one parent is leaving for the grocery store, the other holds the baby and reassures her that Mommy will return. Over the next couple of years, the baby logs enough experiences to count on the reliability and predictability of her parents' availability, as well as to form the cognitive capacities that allow her to understand time, place and the use of other caregivers for support.

Parents usually actively work on plans for separations for childcare transitions. The strategies that help a baby or toddler start a new childcare setting are the same as those that help a child manage other types of separations. Short practice separations at the new location in which the caregiver returns as promised can build the child's confidence. Showing pictures of the caregiver or holding an object of the parent until his return helps the child have confidence that she is remembered while the parent is away.

Short-term separations

Babies and toddlers are extremely sensitive to changes in the consistency of their primary caregivers and their routines. By virtue of her underdeveloped network of neurons, a baby doesn't have any cognitive resources to understand separations from primary caregiver, even when temporary. All a baby knows is that the persons, routines and/or interactions to which she has grown accustomed and relies on are changed.

Even when separations are considered temporary and positive by parents—for example taking a week's vacation without the baby to celebrate a wedding anniversary or a job promotion—these disruptions are problematic for the 12-month-old. The baby has difficulty understanding why, when she cries in the middle of the night, grandma appears instead of her mom.

Our adult minds have visual images of calendars, airplanes, medical procedures or visitation schedules. The minds of infants do not. We may think that a baby is too young to know the difference in caregivers and flexible enough not to be impacted by change, we've found this is not true. Even temporary changes or separations from primary caregivers result in distress that can be exhibited by feeding or sleeping difficulties or general "fussiness"—and nothing alternative caregivers do seems to help.

Extended travel

Many families in this current economy are changing schedules so that parents can work overtime, manage two jobs or travel extensively. We often view these adjustments as temporary and we try to get our families to buckle down and get through the change. But we often underestimate the physical and emotional toll these changes take on us and our children. And, since each child's reaction relates to his age and experience, the strategies that help one child don't necessarily work with a younger or older sibling.

After they finally purchased their dream home, Anika's husband Tejas has been assigned to work on a construction site 200 miles away. The job assignment was too good to pass up, particularly since the construction industry had experienced significant set backs in recent years. Tejas leaves early on Monday mornings and is away from home during the entire week. He arrives home late Friday night, after the children are asleep.

Anika's and Tejas's three children, ages 5, 3 and 1, are having a hard time with Tejas's unavailability. During the week, the 3-year-old refuses to listen to his mom and asks constantly to call his dad. His teachers at the preschool are concerned because he is hitting other children. At home, Anika is constantly refereeing sibling arguments as she tries to keep up with the family's needs. Bedtimes are extremely difficult. A few times a month, the baby will be wakened by her siblings fighting or because they purposefully go into her room and wake her up. Anika's once-flawless routines have disappeared and she struggles to manage the daily duties and needs of her children, who expect two parents to be available.

Saturday mornings, when Tejas is home, is a circus of behaviors. Every issue gets big reactions from the children, both positive and negative. The 5- and 3-year-olds vacillate between hyper-excitement and massive tantrums. The baby clings to Anika and screams if Tejas tries to hold her. Tejas is wondering if it would be less disruptive if he just didn't come home on the weekends.

Hospitalization

Hospitalizations, chemical dependency treatment or unexpected separations, particularly when the child is between 6 and 30 months old, can heighten the child's anxiety, especially when alternative caregivers are not part of her standard routine. By age 3, children are better prepared to generalize their attachment relationships and rely on less familiar caregivers for support. When separations also increase the worry or psychological availability of other primary caregivers, for example when the parent who is away is suffering a major illness or is in jail, the impact for the child can be more intense and last longer because the emotional availability of alternative caregivers may be compromised.

Even with an alternative caregiver's vigilant care, the parent-child relationship may not return to security when baby and caregiver are reunited. The parent may be eager to reconnect with his baby, then feel heartbroken when she refuses to be held. Often, a young child will give the returning caregiver the cold shoulder, usually in response to her internal worry that the parent will again disappear or her anger at being abandoned. A parent may experience rejection as well as guilt over the separation and, without support and understanding, may resort to indifference and downgrade the sense of her own importance in her child's life.

Having more than one responsive, consistent caregiver in a baby's life can ease the adverse effects of caregiver-child separation, in the event that one caregiver's availability changes. When the remaining adult(s) is familiar to the baby, understands the fussiness and can provide consistent, sensitive care, a baby can adapt to a change in caregivers. But a baby needs her caregiver to provide the kind of consistency she has lost and to realize that she can neither understand nor manage her feelings by herself.

After a significant separation, a baby will have a heightened sensitivity to any new separation, no matter how ordinary. The remaining caring adults must keep her routine as consistent as possible, mark transitions with "good-byes" and "hellos," use security items like a blanket or teddy bear for reassurance and minimize the number of caregiver transitions. There are a variety of strategies that can be used to help maintain the connection between the baby and the departed caregiver, including photos, tape recordings and videoconferencing.

The goal of all of these "extras" is to make sure that the disrupted relationship with the primary caregiver does not overwhelm the child's foundation of security and sense of trust. This initial chink can grow into a gaping hole in the child's sense of confidence if she becomes worried that every caring adult might disappear.

Deployment

While military families are resourceful and capable of managing deployment, reunion and redeployment, the demands of these activities during pregnancy and parenting a new baby without a spouse present or while serving on active-duty understandably can result in added challenges in handling everyday routines and experiences (Williams & Rose, 2009). Imagine the emotional strain of giving birth while your husband is deployed to a combat zone, entrusting your other children's overnight care to anyone other than the most trusted friend or family member. A familiar way to manage these unpredictable situations may be to deny the emotional toll by focusing on doing what is necessary as a military family.

For women who have been in active service, the sense of self in combat and that of being a mother may be difficult to reconcile. A study of active-duty, low-risk pregnant women reported that 24 percent of the 97 women surveyed screened positive for prepartum depression, and nearly half of these women said they had considered suicide (O'Boyle, Magann, Ricks, Doyle, & Morrison, 2005).

New technology, particularly the availability of video-chat, helps the deployed parent stay in touch with the day-to-day development of his baby. There are many heartwarming videos on YouTube of fathers watching the birth of their child or toddlers kissing the computer screen. But the day-to-day interactions that build secure and trusting relationships can't happen until the parent is physically present for long periods of time. Following deployment, the military spouse is often eager to jump in as an equal partner in parenting, only to discover that his toddler responds to him more as if he were a kind stranger. The parent who has been at home with the family anticipates the freedom of shared parenting, only to discover that her children remain dependent on her for all primary care.

From the perspective of both the very young child and her parents, the disruption and challenges to early parenting and the parent-child relationship are significant and often underestimated. By acknowledging the significant stress that military parents may experience and recognizing and tapping into their internal and community resources, we can help families develop strong relationships that support the development of their infants and toddlers.

Separation and divorce

To promote healthy development and sturdy parent-child relationships, infants and toddlers whose parents are separated or divorced need frequent, reliable and low-conflict time with each parent. Each parent must convey stability, sensitivity and nurturance so that the very young child knows that both parents care for him and are available despite the changes in the parent's living arrangements. The child's sense of security comes from consistent, predictable, day-to-day interactions with the parent. Weekly or sporadic visits do not allow a baby to gain the sense of certainty and trust necessary to maintain a secure and protective parent-child relationship. For young children, it is not so much about "quality time" but about the quantity of sensitive and engaged parenting that can reduce the negative effects of separation for the child and the parent.

In situations in which the shared parenting role is fraught with conflict, the impact on both parent-child relationships and on the child's development can be compromised. Unfortunately, our court system often looks at the child as property, forgetting that from the child's point of view and development, some arrangements can cause harm.

"I became pregnant in high school and the father of my baby did not support me during the pregnancy and visited the baby only twice after he was born. Now that my son is 18 months old, his father would like to be involved in his life. Because he now lives 1,200 miles away from my son and me, he petitioned the court for visitation. The court recommended that, because of the distance, our son alternate between spending four weeks with his father, whom he doesn't know, and four weeks with me. The guardian ad litem involved in the legal case openly admits that he has no background in child development."

We know it is better for children to have their fathers involved in their lives (barring violence or other significant issues). Working towards a solution that can allow the child to have both parents in his life long-term, free from conflict, is in the child's best interest.

Unfortunately, adult choices, relationships and preferences, as well as the legal structure, don't always create resolutions that are in the child's best interest. Long-standing conflict, old wounds and poor communication can stand in the way of parents working together to find a resolution that accommodates lifestyles of both families and keeps the child's best interest paramount. Because of the intensity of feelings about the child, these situations can quickly dissolve into a parental battle to "win." There's one sure loser, however: the child.

The legal system, while sometimes the last resort to resolve conflict, is often a difficult place to make the child's best interest the key to decisions. The perspective of the baby is overshadowed by a long history of legal tradition that focuses on parental rights, which essentially establish children as property. As you may have discovered, judges, attorneys and guardians ad litem come with their own biases about the flexibility and adaptability of young children.

We need to rethink how our system serves very young children and advocate for using the question: "How will the baby understand (see) it?" Together, we can encourage people to shift to viewing the issues from the baby's perspective, letting go of more entrenched and less helpful conflicts.

Parental Mental Illness

Pregnancy, childbirth and parenting are thought of as times of great joy and celebration, but they are also accompanied by a myriad of emotions that may be unfamiliar, confusing and worrisome to both mother and care provider. Even the most competent mother contends with powerful moments of uncertainty, discontentment and rejection of her role or relationship with her baby. Yet, while most mothers experience maternal ambivalence in varying degrees, few mothers or providers feel prepared to discuss these intense and contradictory feelings.

> Upon the birth of her first child, Lynn left a successful business career for life as a full-time mother. In what seemed like the best compensation for having given up her career, she poured endless energy into preparing for the baby, creating an ideal home and thinking about activities she would do with her baby. Three months after the birth of her daughter, Lynn found these exhausting efforts were less than intrinsically rewarding. While enjoying the benefits of a satisfying marriage and a financially comfortable lifestyle, she was perplexed when unexpected feelings of guilt and despair emerged. During lunch with other women from her pregnancy support group, she announced, "This job is terrible! There are no coffee breaks and I am constantly on-call." Studying the looks on the other mothers' faces, it became clear to Lynn that while they laughed politely, these women were not prepared to offer more support to her rather unattractive feelings. It seemed to her some of the women were having difficulty reconciling their picture of her as a loving and educated mother with that of someone who talked openly about her mixed feelings towards motherhood. Left to sift through her feelings on her own, Lynn wondered if something about her was amiss.

Whether we know it or not, we all carry preconceived notions about motherhood—of what a mother should be, how she should approach her role and how she should handle her responsibilities. From an early age, children are filled with images of "good mothers" and "bad mothers." These icons grace the covers of magazines, are embroidered in fairytales and fill primetime television viewing. For many women like Lynn, hoping to discuss the unexpected and unappealing feelings of motherhood produces considerable tension between seeking support and being labeled by family or friends as a bad mother.

The response of the mothers in Lynn's parenting circle reveals and reinforces the societal unacceptability of forging into these waters. Until now, voicing ambivalent or resentful feelings as a mother has been seen as a demonstration of personal or parenting flaws. After all, mothers are innately loving and unconditionally accepting, right?

Maternal ambivalence is typical, particularly under stressful circumstances, but it is essential that providers feel prepared to distinguish between the conditions that allow a mother to tolerate her ambivalent feelings without compromising her capacity to care for her child, and those conditions that foster the mother's neglect and maltreatment of her baby. Specifically a provider's understanding and acceptance that maternal ambivalence is common that will assist a parent in acknowledging and managing negative feelings. By doing so, the provider becomes a powerful ally in supporting the mother-child relationship. For example, when the mother has inadequate support, little knowledge of child development and limited personal resources, the task of overcoming and understanding her ambivalence is far more complicated and worrisome.

> Under the covers of a standard hospital bed in an inner-city hospital sits 16-year-old Lisa, who has just given birth to a healthy 7-pound baby girl. Having kept her pregnancy secret until 30 weeks gestation, she now cowers in her nightgown, refusing to look at or feed her baby. Lisa is scheduled to return home with her infant in less than 24 hours, and a worried staff nurse calls the school social worker who has been working with Lisa since her pregnancy was discovered. The nurse complains, "I don't think Lisa really wants to learn how to take care of her baby."

Personal challenges of substance abuse, untreated depression, other mental illness, teenage pregnancy and domestic violence can compromise a mother's ability to make choices in the best interest of her baby. In these situations, unaddressed feelings of maternal ambivalence can undermine or distort a mother's hopes and expectations for her relationship with her child. Without support or assistance, she is left in a position to direct these powerful negative feelings towards her baby, at times resulting in serious and life-threatening consequences.

> Arriving at the home of Jenny, a 24-year-old single mother of two, the visiting public health nurse found Jenny and her 4-year-old daughter coloring a picture at the table in the dimly lit kitchen. Lying in a crib in a dark room at the opposite end of the house, with a bottle propped by blankets, was Darla, a 10-month-old who was both sight- and hearing-impaired. In response to the nurse's concern that the baby was being neglected, Jenny said, "It doesn't matter because she can't see or hear me anyway." The baby was beginning to lose weight and was at risk of being diagnosed with Failure to Thrive.

When extreme ambivalence goes unchecked, the overt or covert maltreatment of the baby appears to the mother as an acceptable way of dealing with these deeply disturbing emotions. In such situations, a provider must be prepared to address not only the immediate neglect or maltreatment of a child, but also the source and extent of the mother's ambivalence. In order to do so, providers must have access to effective strategies for helping mothers manage the tremendous tasks of parenthood, particularly when the mother struggles to manage her own emotions and vulnerabilities.

Maternal Depression in Early Parenting

> "After five years of infertility and multiple miscarriages, our first child was born three months ago. He is an easygoing baby and we are delighted to have him in our

lives. However, I am not enjoying motherhood. After my first two miscarriages, I was treated for depression. Now, my body and spirit feel the same as when I was depressed. Why would I be depressed when we finally have our healthy baby boy?"

Experiencing the "baby blues" following childbirth is a typical part of the experience. Sharing the highs and lows of this experience with supportive partners is an important part of the process. Even the most competent mother contends with powerful moments of uncertainty, discontent and rejection of her role or relationship with her baby. Having a newborn in the home often results in sleep deprivation and social isolation, which can have serious consequences and effects on feelings and thinking. Accepting help from others, taking naps when the opportunity arises and reengaging in favorite activities can help combat the drain of energy related to having a newborn.

Because baby blues is a temporary condition, strategies for helping a mother manage her experience are typically found in her environment and within her support system. A woman with a new baby needs trusted relationships in which she can express these intimate experiences and feelings, including those with her family, friends and medical provider. Joining a parent support group, confiding in a friend or reading the memoirs of other mothers may help.

Sometimes, however, pregnancy and the transition to parenting a new baby can result in a longer-lasting depression. Women who have experienced depression at other times in their lives have a greater probability for developing depression during or following pregnancy. Recent studies demonstrate that 10 to 14 percent of all pregnant and postpartum women experience clinical depression (Wisner et al, 2013). The likelihood of depression increases for teenage mothers, women of color and those living in poverty or those who experience high levels of stress.

Mothers suffering from depression not surprisingly, experience more anxiety and stress in their parenting roles than mothers who enjoy responsive and engaged parent-child relations. Over time, their children experience fewer positive emotions and even show distress in situations that most other children find pleasurable.

It is the middle of the afternoon and Maggie is lying on the couch. She intended to get up and change her clothes, but fatigue overtook her and she fell back to sleep after propping a bottle for her 5-month-old son Mark. Lying on the blanket at the foot of the couch, Mark begins to whimper. Maggie leans over and, without looking, pushes one of the figures dangling from the toy bar hanging over Mark. He looks toward the swinging figure, then at his hands. From there, his gaze travels toward the glow of the television. He is silent.

A few mornings later, Maggie feels well enough to take a shower and makes a plan in her head about how to spend the day playing with Mark. After showering, intense feelings of mental and physical exhaustion begin to overwhelm her. But before retreating in her robe to the couch for a brief nap, she sits on the floor next to Mark, who is in his car seat. She forces herself to smile at him and begins to sing. He looks toward her lips briefly and then turns his head toward the television. Maggie's belief that she is a bad parent is reinforced and her feelings intensify with Mark's lack of interest.

FROM THE BABY'S POINT OF VIEW

Mark is not used to interacting and unable to respond with confidence and interest to his mother's attempts to engage him. For months, his bids for attention or new discoveries have been ignored. He does not know how to respond or have the "expected" interactions skills.

Depression affects a woman's thinking, moods, sleep patterns and health, and may compromise her feelings and reactions towards herself, her baby and her family. A woman experiencing depression may have more difficulty managing her daily routine if she is overwhelmed by feelings of sadness, agitation, guilt and worry. The baby is more likely to nap during the day, be difficult to get to sleep at night and experience more frequent night-waking—an issue for both mom and baby. Depression can be worsened by lack of sleep—or even partly triggered by it.

While she may struggle to maintain a loving and concerned attitude towards her baby, prolonged, untreated depression can ultimately interfere with her ability to sensitively respond to her baby, which in turn has the potential to affect the child's development. The new mother needs to contact her health professional and engage in effective treatment. Overall, it is important to understand that depression is not something a woman can get over on her own, nor is it a flaw or a sign of being a bad parent.

Screening for depression is relatively easy and gives the parent the opportunity to discover which combination and intensity of symptoms are considered unusual (Breedlove, G. & Fryzelka, 2011). Depression can vary in duration and severity, but is typically hallmarked by the loss of interest in or ability to complete everyday activities, which may include taking care of the baby in the case of a depressed mom, and by overwhelming intense feelings of sadness and/or anxiety. A woman will not usually experience all of the listed symptoms, but any symptom listed below that is causing distress should be considered significant and appropriate screening and treatment pursued.

The range of possible symptoms may include:
• Sadness.
• Lack of interest in caring for self, baby or family including nurturing, feeding, and communicating.
• A sense of lack of control or feelings of being trapped without options to change or meet one's own needs.
• Sleeplessness and restlessness even when the baby is sleeping.

- A sense of being restless, unable to relax and the inability to find ways to feel calm.
- Overwhelming anger, frustration and rage, sometimes resulting from the persistent needs of the baby.
- Persistent feelings of wanting to hurt the baby, wishing the baby had not come, or wanting to find someone else to care for the baby.

Depression is manageable and treatable and effective interventions for depression during pregnancy, childbirth and parenting are available. A woman experiencing these symptoms should not be dissuaded from seeking appropriate treatment, either by her hope that she can solve these feelings on her own or by others who tell her she will be fine in a few weeks. Together, she and her physician can determine the components of treatment, including the benefits of medication, counseling and activities. With appropriate treatment, the symptoms of depression can be managed, allowing a woman to return to the typical and everyday experiences of motherhood.

Treatment of depression is not only important for the mother's responsiveness to her baby but ultimately for the healthy development of the child. Many studies have demonstrated that maternal depression negatively impacts the regulation of affect and of physiological patterns of infants (Carter et al, 2001; Laurent, et al, 2013). The data suggests that maternal depression during the baby's first year, may lead to more negative temperament that impacts later development and may predispose the child for later mental health difficulties (Field, 1995; Talge, Neal & Glover, 2007). Behavior problems in children during preschool and elementary school are associated with maternal depression in a child's first year of life (O'Conner et al, 2002).

One promising finding is that breastfeeding seems to improve the dyadic relationships as well as safeguard the infants of mothers experiencing depression from experiencing affective and physiological dysregulation (Jones, McFall, & Diego, 2004).

Paternal Depression

Postpartum depression in mothers has become more widely discussed and diagnosed in recent years; it's less understood that fathers can and do go through pre- or postpartum depression that also impacts the development of their children. Typically, we think of depression as sadness or tearfulness, but men are less likely to acknowledge these symptoms. When talking about depression in men, symptom descriptions need to include irritability, emotional withdrawal and feelings of detachment. Sleep deprivation, which can alter a person's neurochemical balance, can trigger depression in some men who may have had underlying risk factors or previously unrecognized symptoms.

> "My wife delivered our first child three weeks ago. I feel like there is something wrong with me because I don't feel an overwhelming connection with my son. My wife is breastfeeding, so it seems like the only thing I can do with him is change his diaper—which I really don't like. I want to be a great dad but I feel lost."

A recent study in Norway that followed the development of more than 30,000 children found that a very low number of fathers (3 percent) scored high on measures of anxiety and depression during the second trimester of pregnancy. However, if a father experienced mental health symptoms, his children were significantly more likely to significant emotional and behavioral difficulties at age 3 (Kvalevagg et al, 2013).

Depression postpartum is common in fathers as well as in mothers of young children and is most common during the first year of their children's lives, usually spiking when the baby is 3 to 6 months old. The statistics for postpartum depression in men is the same as in women, about one in 10. However, that estimate increases significantly (25 to 50 percent) if the mothers also are experiencing postpartum depression (Goodman, 2004). Translating these findings, five out of every 100 newborns have two parents who are experiencing depressive symptoms during their critical first year of life.

Because the impact on the quality of maternal care is more visible, paternal depression has received relatively little attention, yet it significantly impacts the development of children. In a prospective study, researchers found that depression in fathers during the postnatal period, eight weeks after delivery, increased the chances of behavioral problems in children at 3½ years and increased the risk for boys of being diagnosed with conduct disorders at age 7 (Paulson & Bazemore, 2010; Ramchandni, et al, 2008). These findings were independent of depression in mothers. Children of fathers who were depressed also demonstrated poorer language skills.

When depressed, fathers demonstrate less sensitivity and warmth in parenting and an increase in conflict, hostility and feelings of rejection. Fathers suffering from depressive symptoms during the first year of their children's lives are less likely to read to their babies and more likely to resort to spanking—an inappropriate strategy that has significantly harmful effects, particularly when used with a baby (Davis, Davis, Freed, & Clark, 2011). Paternal depression is also associated with higher unemployment and increased use of illicit or prescription drugs or alcohol, which can have devastating effects on the financial health of the family and further exacerbate relationship conflicts.

Reponses to parental mental illness

When parents themselves are having difficulty maintaining relationships, experiencing a full range of emotions—including joy— and finding learning overly taxing, special consideration needs to be made to safeguard the development of the baby and the relationship between the baby and parent. The child needs responsive, sensitive attention and care as the parent is recovering. The worst situation for the baby and the mom is for the infant to spend each of his days on the blanket on the floor next to the couch where mom lies and the television is the only stimulation for both of them. The child needs active interactions so that he can develop the capacities that will make him a good partner and easier to parent.

Maltreatment and Foster Care

Maltreatment that occurs in a baby's home interrupts her sense of personal safety, trust in others and outlook on the future. Physical harm and/or neglect of a very young child is happening at a time in which the parent-child relationship and brain development are setting the pathway and architecture for the rest of the child's life (Cicchetti & Toth, 2000; NCR, 2000). Research has found that consequences of maltreatment, particularly for infants and toddlers, can be devastating. Protecting children and making sure their environment is safe is equally as important as making sure they have the capacities and opportunity to develop secure relationships with consistent and sensitive adults.

The largest age group entering the foster care system is that of children under age 4 (Cohen, Cole & Szrom, 2011). This is significant, given that that's the age at which stability and availability of relationships is most central to healthy development and most foster care practices consist of a series of temporary, unpredictable and short-term separation-reunion cycles. The emotional and developmental harm of separation can confound the impact of the initial maltreatment, unless specific attention is paid to maintaining close and frequent connections with parents, helping foster parents recognize and adjust to the specific ways in which infants and toddlers show distress and intervention services specifically designed to improve child and parent outcomes long-term.

> Josephina was placed at birth with a caring and sensitive foster mother and father in their 60s who had raised five children of their own. Reunited with her mother when she was 4 months old, Josephina was placed at 8 months of age with the same foster parents when her mother relapsed and began using heroin again.
>
> Josephina's response to being in foster care was relatively positive. She quickly adapted to the sleep schedule her

foster parents developed for her, ate well and began to freely explore in their child-friendly home.

Unfortunately for Josephina, a month after placement, her foster father was taken by ambulance to the hospital after suffering what would be diagnosed as a debilitating stroke. Overwhelmed by the needs of her husband, Josephina's foster mother regretfully asked for Josephina to be moved to another foster home.

At the new foster home, Josephina seemed disoriented and inconsolably sad. The new foster parent, who had three elementary-age children of her own, initially gave Josephina extra attention but quickly became weighed down and annoyed by her continual demand to be held and her ongoing inconsolability. After several weeks with no change in her behaviors, the new foster mother began to ignore Josephina's constant cries for attention, believing that the previous foster parents gave her too much attention and that she needed to get used to being part of a bigger family.

FROM THE BABY'S POINT OF VIEW

Josephina wandered around the new house. It smelled and sounded different. She searched for her foster mother and foster father; like her mother, they had disappeared. She did not know the people in the new house. She didn't feel like eating or playing. She only cried.

Unfortunately, our foster care system was built for school-age children, who understand the parenting mistakes made and what needs to be changed to keep them safe, whose concept of time includes knowledge of what once-a-week visits, "temporary" shelter or reunification means. An older child carries with her images (both good and bad) and the presence of her parents while separated. None of these skills is available to an infant or toddler.

Close collaboration between child protective services and early intervention has been mandated in the Keeping Children and Families Safe Act of 2003. Community-based services can provide a high level of support for child and parent.

> While her mother slept on the couch and her baby brother played in the playpen, 3-year-old Maria turned off the television and walked out the front door of her family's townhouse. Knowing exactly where she was going, Maria used an elevated sidewalk to cross a busy street, marched into the building in which her childcare was located and opened the door to her classroom, greeting her teachers with a smile.

> The staff, while alarmed that no parent was with Maria, welcomed her into the classroom. A phone call to child protective services soon followed. When mom did not answer the center director's call, the home visitor went to the townhouse and found mom on the couch, depressed and self-medicating with alcohol.

> Because the center director had worked with the police on other child-protection issues, non-uniformed officers arrived to handle the situation, parking at the back of the building. The director prepared Maria for their arrival, giving her one of the blankets that she uses for naptime and comfort. She also reassured her that these adults would help her mom and take care of her baby brother.

> When the case was presented in court, the judge was surprised to see that the home visitor from the childcare center who had reported the maltreatment issue was

at the mother's side. With a strong explanation of the center's philosophy about supporting the relationships between children and the important adults in their lives, the home visitor asked the judge to allow the children to continue attending the center while in foster care. In return, the center would provide a location for supervised family visits and would continue to support the mother's efforts to better care for her children and resolve the protection issues.

With this plan in place, the mother visited her children while they were in foster care every other day, getting together with them in a familiar setting—their childcare. In six weeks, the mother had completed a drug treatment program, was receiving therapy for depression and had finished her protection plan. The family was reunited.

Maria's story demonstrates the crucial role that childcare can play in the lives of young children and families who are at greatest risk, including children in the child welfare system, children in poverty and children with disabilities. At a time of family disruption, childcare can provide a familiar setting, well-known routines and nurturing and consistent relationships. A high quality, neighborhood-based center like Baby's Space, which Maria attends, offers a strategic location for effective prevention and intervention efforts. While parents work to provide better care for their children, continued involvement and coordination with center staff provides the support critical for helping children manage significant family crises with the least amount of additional harm. When her mother was asleep on the couch, Maria knew where to go to find caring and nurturing adults: her classroom.

Significant childhood adversity without the protection of responsive, consistent and sensitive primary caregivers alters the architecture of developing brains and increases the risk of physical and mental health disorders. When there is neglect or maltreatment, a young child needs a team of familiar, responsive and caring adults to counterbalance the impact of maltreatment and family separation. Babies can succeed even during the most difficult times when caring adults provide consistent love and support with opportunities for engagement and learning.

Personal challenges of substance abuse, untreated depression, teen pregnancy and domestic—like those of Maria's mother—can compromise a parent's ability to make choices that are in the best interest of her children. She may lack a support network of friends and family. She may have experienced violence. Without ongoing support or assistance, she is left to direct her powerful negative feelings toward her baby, at times resulting in serious and life-threatening consequences.

Childcare centers that provide holistic, full-spectrum services including home visits, monthly family events and parent education activities in one-on-one and group settings, can improve the health and well-being of children by helping parents strengthen their abilities to adequately care for and nurture them. The U.S. Department of Health and Human Services' Children's Bureau identifies the five protective factors linked to secure attachment as: commitment to nurturing and attachment, child development knowledge, parent resilience, social connections and concrete support. The staff at a childcare center can help parents work on these protective factors over several years, not just at the time of a crisis.

More than 70 percent of Minnesota mothers are employed and the welfare subsidy to stay home to raise young children has been eliminated, making childcare an essential partner in the rearing of young children. When funded at levels that can retain quality staff and maintain low child-to-teacher ratios, childcare can provide essential security and consistency for very young children. The integration of parent education, advocacy and mental health services within the childcare setting offers the best opportunity of success for parents struggling with trauma, unexpected transitions or parenting difficulties.

All children deserve a healthy start to life. We can take a profound step toward addressing the adverse impact of maltreatment and subsequent involvement of the child-protective system by making it a matter of policy and practice to nurture and protect the primary relationships of children—with family members and those who provide childcare.

6

"You make my feelings cry."
3-year-old

MENTAL HEALTH READINESS

If a child has a sore throat, we take him to see the pediatrician and are happy to use amoxicillin or another antibiotic to deal with his illness. Does she have ear infection after another? Maybe it's time for a more serious medical intervention, the insertion of tubes to drain excess fluid and reduce the likelihood of infection.

But when it comes to mental health, we are hesitant to acknowledge that very young children may need help; they don't always "grow out of it." In fact, initial mental health issues may make it more difficult for the adults in a child's life to interact and respond effectively with the child, decreasing the likelihood of success for that child.

There are ways to assess and recognize mental health in very young children, just as there are ways to assess and recognize physical health. And there are strategies and treatments that can give every child a better start on life.

"When our children see us expressing our emotions,
they can learn that their own feelings are natural and
permissible, can be expressed, and can be talked about.
That's an important thing for our children to learn."
Fred Rogers

I am a baby nerd. Watching, talking, and playing with a baby makes my heart sing. Almost always I am looking for how the baby shows interest in the world, participates in relationships and demonstrate happiness. Why? Because a baby's behavior tells us volumes.

On a day when the infant room was exceptionally busy, I volunteered to take 4-month-old Dante. In our family lounge, I sat with him on my lap and immediately started looking for eye contact and his social smile. I couldn't get him to make eye contact. Trying a number of strategies and positions, I finally tipped his head down as I held his body. His eyes met mine and he smiled. I sat him up on my lap—no eye contact, no smile. Tipped him back down—eye contact and a lovely smile.

Dante could make eye contact and smile in response to social engagement, but not while looking at me from a seated position. I supported him in a standing position and crouched my head down low so that I was looking up at him. The result: He smiled while looking at me.

After examining his body positions, I went back into the classroom to ask the teachers if they had ever noticed anything odd about the position of Dante's head. They too had noticed that his head looked like it was not quite centered. I asked them to check with mom, who was relieved to hear that she was not a bad mom for thinking her baby's head was on crooked.

> After checking with Dante's pediatrician, his 17-year-old mom was able to teach the teachers about his condition and demonstrate the physical therapy exercises that would help him. Infant torticollis, which literally means twisted neck, is a condition results in the infant tilting his head in one direction. It may take up to three months after birth to develop. For Dante, his preferred direction was down. With diagnosis and treatment, the teaching staff was able to join Dante's mom in strengthening his range of motion while adjusting his positions to allow him to fully engage in relationships and learning.

Dante's ultimate diagnosis was about a physical impairment, but we discovered it by looking for emotional capacities. I would like to think that our infant teachers and the mom were not far behind me in noticing and wondering why he did not make eye contact easily. Nevertheless, I can only imagine if they did not speak up and it was not until his 6-month check-up that the pediatrician made the diagnosis. The unintended loss of opportunities for building relationships and communication could have led to difficulties in Dante's development and in his relationship with his mom.

A baby's cognitive, physical and emotional developments, by virtue of the exquisite role of relationships and experience, are intricately intertwined. Dante's abilities to achieve a calm and interested state and to form and be interested in relationships are as vitally important as being able to roll over or sit up. In fact, these motor accomplishments require these emotional capacities. But in typical settings, how do parents notice what is not typical and where do parents go for advice or when concerned about their children's development?

Parents' Concerns About Mental Health

For a year, I kept a blog that let parents, grandparents and teachers write to me with questions about the social and emotional development of their children. The majority of the questions were about three main areas: eating, sleeping and toileting. What these topics have in common is that they represent the point at which parents discover that their child is an active and independent partner—both cooperative and uncooperative. Most parents learn that they can't force a child to sleep, or eat or poop. There are dozens of parent-help books that take on these challenges with prescribed routines and strategies, but parents still struggle.

For the blog, my answers followed a similar pattern: validating the difficulties of parenting young children, providing a developmental context and suggesting ways to understand the meaning of behavior. Thinking of behavior as "meaning" rather than something that needs to be managed is a different way to look at child development and parenting. Understanding that a baby is not a blank slate to be molded but rather a dynamic partner in his own development engages parents' curiosity and drive to understand their child's experiences.

In creating the blog, I was curious about the kinds of challenges parents were experiencing and how to create concise and supportive responses in a condensed format. Some of the questions were commonplace.

> "Perhaps a month ago, our 21-month-old began waking up in the middle of the night (not unusual) and, instead of going back to sleep, throwing her baba out of the crib (unusual). She cries and pleads (mama, dada, baba...) with us to get it for her. My wife has observed this behavior and is pretty sure it's not accidental. We've tried to ignore these episodes (easier said than done) or have, on occasion, sternly reprimanded her for throwing baba. But it still continues—not every night, but often enough that my wife and I are sleep-deprived."

In response to questions, I often suggested that parents use only strategies they were committed to and only when they have the time, energy and support to make the change. It may not help to start a new nighttime routine when one parent is going to be traveling, houseguests are expected or a major holiday is approaching. When a parent is inconsistent and gives in to whining or tantrums, they decrease the likelihood that the strategy will be successful. Slot machines pay winnings on an intermittent reinforcement schedule. Children, like gamblers, know that the more they persist, the more likely they are to get what they want.

Some of the questions required that the parents examine their own beliefs about parenting and the nature of their child's distress. Children can be the barometers for issues that adults are reluctant to address or that relate to their own experiences of being parented.

> "My father- and mother-in-law handle my 2-year-old's tantrums in what I consider unhelpful ways. They are frustrated by his tantrums and they show it by taunting him while he is fussing, saying, 'Waah, waah.'

> "Sometimes they bring up past tantrums, even when he is being cooperative. They say things like, 'Remember that tantrum you had before nap last time? You were a bad boy.'

> "And sometimes they tease him and actually cause a tantrum by bringing up things they can't/won't deliver: 'Want to try some wine? Too bad, you can't have it.' Now, if we are going to their home for Sunday night dinner, my son starts crying or hides in his room."

FROM THE BABY'S POINT OF VIEW

Josiah doesn't understand teasing. He sees his grandparents laughing but feels hurt by their words. Trying to be good, he resists sitting next to his grandparents. He doesn't know when he can trust their words and when they will make him feel bad. (Teasing and other types of passive-aggressive behaviors are difficult for children and adults alike to understand.)

Children learn at an early age which adults are supportive and can be trusted. Most parents need to be reassured that their interactions as parents are the most important in their child's development of self-esteem and confidence, even with complicated family dynamics. But children are not invulnerable. Parents have critical roles as interpreters and protectors. From the child's perspective, the parents' response, even if it is to do nothing, sends a message about trust, relationships, feelings and empathy. It is easy for adults to brush off these interactions, saying it's an adult's kidding or that the child is too young to notice, or to negatively ascribe characteristics to the child, such as being oversensitive or a "mama's boy." From the child's perspective, crying and hiding in anticipation of a visit are strong signals of the impact and the need for protection.

Sometimes the questions came from providers who felt unprepared to help families with the magnitude or complexity of the problems.

A parent in our program shared that her 3-year-old son "stomped to death" several bunnies in their backyard. The experience was horrifying for this mother, as she has never seen her son act so violently before. This mother believes an older, more aggressive cousin, who also contributed to killing the bunnies, influenced her son.

In the classroom, her son is very compliant, soft spoken and gentle. I understand that this mother experienced domestic violence in the past and the son witnessed it. Should we be concerned or is hurting small animals developmentally appropriate for a young child?

In this case, while the older cousin may have had some influence over the younger boy's actions, the 3-year-old had the actual experience of killing. Ideally, the young child—with the support of caring adults—would participate in relevant consequences for his actions such as burying or participating in a culturally appropriate ceremony for the animals. He would also benefit from opportunities to talk, write and draw about his feelings both during and after the incident. But developing and implementing these strategies would typically call for professional mental health support.

"Because the young child feels with such intensity, he experiences sorrows that seem inconsolable and losses that feel unbearable. A precious toy gets broken or a good-bye cannot be endured. When this happens, words like 'sad' or 'disappointed' seem a travesty because they cannot possibly capture the enormity of the child's loss. He needs a loving adult presence to support him in his pain but he does not want to be talked out of it."

Alicia Lieberman, PhD

MENTAL HEALTH SCREENING

How do parents know when to seek a therapist and when to handle issues on their own? Even with issues far less dramatic, parents wonder, "Is this typical?" Equally important, how do parents assure themselves that their children's development is on target? Early identification of children who may be at risk for mental health disorders is the first step in the diagnostic process. Much like developmental screening, which is an integral and expected part of well-child pediatric visits, screening for potential social and emotional difficulties in very young children is the parents' first step in determining if their children's behaviors are on track developmentally.

For most development and health issues, parents can rely on their primary health care provider. Parents know that their child will receive 11 well-child visits during the first three years of their child's life. At these well-child visits, parents expect their health care provider to: collect data, for example, health history, height, weight; ask them to complete developmental checklists; conduct screenings for vision and hearing; and examine and assess physical functioning of ears, heart and other major organs and systems. Parents also expect to go to their primary care provider for acute or chronic conditions such as ear infections or asthma.

For behavioral issues, such as sleeping and eating, a parent is also likely to turn to the primary care provider. But what tools does the health practitioner use to examine or assess the scope of the problem, particularly if it is a symptom related to the child's emotional capacities or difficulties in the parent-child relationship, in a visit that is scheduled for 10 to 20 minutes?

> "My son doesn't know the meaning of the word sleep," Tara reports at her son's 9-month, well-child visit. Her voice is a monotone and her affect is flat.
>
> After looking over his developmental screening and completing the physical examination, the pediatrician says to Tara, "Well, that just might be the way he is. Some children need less sleep."
>
> That afternoon, when her son refuses to take a nap, Tara, overwhelmed with exhaustion, puts him in his crib and leaves him wailing for 60 minutes while she goes into the yard to pull dandelions. She is beginning to resent the day he came into her life.

It's true that the tantrum-prone toddler can emerge a year later as a communicative, cooperative preschooler thanks to developing his capacity for communication, cognition and self-regulation. We've all seen this happen. On the other hand, we've all seen signs of disturbance, delay or disorder in young children that persist even when we wish they wouldn't. We hate to acknowledge that trauma, or a misstep in emotional development that if caught early, could avoid later difficulties.

But there is no way for any clinician, no matter how well skilled, to "eyeball" social and emotional development. Starting at a young age, the behavior of a child in a well-child visit can be consumed by their worries about getting shots. Parents' expressions of concern can be misinterpreted for a variety of reasons. And in a busy practice, it is easiest to suggest parenting resources or to recommend waiting until the next visit to see if the issue is still a problem. Given the rapid development of children and the wide variety of parenting materials available, these suggestions work most of the time.

What if there is a problem in emotional development that "wait and see" will make worse, or the suggested parenting strategy is in conflict with the family's culture or further compromises the security of the parent-child relationship? Conversely what if a physical problem is a symptom of a mental health problem and expensive and ultimately unnecessary tests are ordered because problems in emotional capacities were never considered? If emotional readiness is at the heart of school readiness, shouldn't all parents and their health care team give the same consideration and evaluation to emotional health as they do to physical health?

With so much interconnection between brain development, physical maturation and emotional capacities, how can we measure the social and emotional competencies of young children and determine if their paths are typical or something about which we should be concerned? We need a reliable and valid screening for social and emotional development comparable to those available for general development. Parent report measures take advantage of the family's knowledge and interest in their child's development. Just as with developmental screenings, they also create the opportunity for parents to learn about what social and emotional skills their child should have at which ages. All parents should have the peace of mind that their child is on track with all aspects of development and that their trusted providers are following when things are different than expected.

A few reliable and valid screening measures to be completed by parents and suitable for a well-child health visit exist. The most commonly used screening tool in primary medical practices, early education settings and home visiting programs for infant and toddler social and emotional development is the parent report measure, Ages and Stages Questionnaire®, Social Emotional (Squires, Bricker, Heo & Twombly, 2001). This screening measure allows parents to monitor their children's development and professionals to determine if there is a risk that requires further evaluation. It takes fifteen to twenty minutes for parents to complete and is available in six-month intervals from 6 months of age to 60 months. The Devereux Early Childhood

Assessment for Infants and Toddlers [DECA-IT®] is similar in length and procedure and is for children 1 to 36 months old. Brief Infant Toddler Social Emotional Assessment [BITSEA®] is a seven- to 10-minute screening tool for children 12 to 36 months old.

Unfortunately, too few children and parents have the opportunity to be reassured of the positive nature of their children's social and emotional trajectory or to have early detection of things not going well. In a Minnesota Children's Mental Health Division survey of children under the age of 3 who are enrolled in public health care, while 93 percent received a primary care visit, only 3 percent received a social emotional screening.

Knowing that the majority of pediatricians want to be responsible for identifying behavioral management problems in young children, Mayo Clinic-Rochester's primary care department, the local school district and the Olmsted County Public Health program formed a partnership for screening very young children. The Ages and Stages Questionnaire: Social-Emotional (ASQ:SE®) was completed by parents of children under the age of 5 who were participating in services or programs. Working collaboratively with community resources, these organizations provided efficient and comprehensive screening. The primary care physicians helped develop a follow-up for children whose screening indicated the need for further assessment. Follow-up plans include: appropriate educational resources and clinician counseling, referral to appropriate community agencies that can diagnose and treat mental health disorders in children or referral to an appropriate medical sub-specialist like a pediatric psychiatrist or developmental pediatrician.

"It is amazing what you are able to do to positively impact
mental health care for young children!"
Brian Lynch, MD

Mental Health Diagnoses in Babies

A reliable screening measure can show parents and teachers that a child is on track, or confirm that those nagging little worries merit a professional evaluation. But for most of us the phrase "mental health in children" conjures the resentful teenage girl who slouches into the psychologist's office or the school-aged child who struggles to maintain focus in the classroom. We're not used to observing toddlers for signs of traumatic stress disorder or monitoring anxiety. We "know" that babies only need to be held and fed and loved by caring adults; their only worry has to do with the timing of their next meal. The very idea of diagnosing a young child with a mental illness can feel like over-reaching.

When a toddler is pulling at his ear, not sleeping well through the night, cranky and running a low-grade fever, a parent calls the clinic for an appointment. She has an idea of the diagnosis—ear infection—and she knows what to expect once she reaches the clinic. She knows that the assessment will involve a physical exam that looks for symptoms of an ear infection, most typically reddening of the ear drum and sometimes fluid. The course of treatment and when to expect symptom relief is also known.

If infections prove to be recurrent, a preventative intervention like tubes decreases the likelihood of long-term hearing loss as a result of chronically inflamed ears. The pediatrician moves ahead with the preventative treatment with the knowledge that by age 5, the anatomic structure of the ear will have changed enough to make future treatment unnecessary. We intervene with an ear infection because it can lead to later hearing loss. Most of us don't question the wisdom of this calm, orderly system of gathering information, diagnosing the problem and prescribing treatment.

But where does a parent go when a toddler is not sleeping

well and cranky for days on end? What if the child's behavior is so unpredictable that the family can no longer go out to a restaurant and dad is happy to go to work in the morning to get relief from being around his child?

Why don't parents have easy access to screening, assessment, diagnosis and treatment of mental health problems? In my experience, the real barrier to diagnosing mental illness in babies is not their inability to sit in our offices and talk about their worries.

It's us.

Too little to be "broken"

Many of us have a vague sense that a child is too young to remember or be impacted by early negative experiences. We want that child to be resilient enough to withstand changes in caregivers, severe poverty or domestic violence. We assure ourselves that the hearts, minds and souls of young children must be resilient and that they can bounce back from early adversity.

The baby is manipulating the parent

We also tend to put young children's behavior in an adult context, attributing to them motives and sneaky agendas that are developmentally beyond their abilities. Our solutions tend to fit older children and underestimate the importance of development.

Blaming the child takes the parent off the hook

Confounding the situation, we see others or ourselves as not good enough parents, making the solution one of changing parents and changing parenting practices without ever examining the source or conditions of the problem. We worry about scapegoating the child, while giving the parents excuses not to deal with their own issues. Parents do have an impact on their children and—under extreme conditions, such as abuse and neglect—can cause substantial harm, but the avalanche of new research tells us that the emotional development of young children is much more than a mirror image or composite of positive or negative parenting. Yet many of us still operate under the assumption that simply improving the quality of a child's parenting would "fix" the child's symptoms.

Why do we have to call it mental illness?

Our cultural unease around acknowledging and diagnosing mental illness in young children often expresses itself as worry—as parents and practitioners—that we'll cause future harm. There are many that believe we have become a problem-focused society rather thank strength-based. We believe that babies are "happy" and will grow out of their problems. We forget that babies are on a developmental trajectory that may make them particularly vulnerable at certain points to conditions that older children and adults can handle better. Certain stressful conditions are toxic to a young child's development.

We shouldn't be medicating babies

Many of us can only imagine mental health diagnosis or treatment with the image of a psychoanalyst, baby on the couch, offering medication to fix the problem. Most of us are familiar with three diagnoses used with children: attention deficit hyperactivity disorder (ADHD), autism and, with rising worries about over-diagnosis, bipolar disorder. Because of our limited experience with mental health, particularly with young children, we worry that medication is the primary treatment option, particularly with the common use of Ritalin and other stimulants.

A label will follow a child forever

Mental health carries a negative and pervasive stigma. Because of the public school systems' use of "labels' to qualify students for special education, there exists an inescapable perception (and perhaps reality) that mental health diagnosis becomes a permanent part of a child's school record. We worry about leaving the mental health office with a child labeled as "mood disordered," "traumatized" or "sleep disordered." No one wants to saddle a toddler with a permanent label or stigma. But just as we know that a special education category (such as Emotionally/Behaviorally Disordered or Learning Disabled) qualifies a child for the educational services he needs today, a psychological diagnosis accomplishes the same thing: it invites early intervention, often making treatment possible.

Will my child be locked up?

Mental health by default becomes a discussion of mental illness. If we look at media for reference, mental illness describes a person whose deeds have caused great harm and threatens society. Mental illness is perceived as permanent and dangerous. Our fears reveal our own internalized prejudices about mental health diagnoses in general. And no matter how much research comes to light, many still perceive mental illness in anyone as a character weakness.

"Early detection and early intervention will give us the best outcomes."
Thomas Insel, MD

Screening, Diagnosis and Treatment

We now know that babies are not blank slates to be filled in by their moms and dads; their emotional health—like ours—is a complex interaction of genetics, behavior and environment. Some babies enter the world with internal capacities that make caregiving challenging even for the most competent of parents. Others' early experiences alter their biological interactions and manifest in troublesome (or positive) behavior. The signs are there; we just need to be willing and able to read them.

> Knowing how special and intense the early days with a newborn can be, Mike and Sophie arranged for Sophie's parents to care for their son Jack, age 2½, for the week following their new baby's birth. Jack had loved his past overnights at his grandparents' house and expressed his excitement. Sophie and Mike prepared Jack well for this full-week stay, even packing a present a day for him to help him track how many "sleeps" he had left at grandma and grandpa's.

> The week went well for everyone: Mike and Sophie bonded with Madeline, their newborn daughter, and reconnected with each other. Jack enjoyed his outings with his grandfather and opening his daily gift. He did resist bedtime more than usual, and asked repeatedly when he would see his parents and new sister. His busy days, however, wore him out and helped him fall asleep quickly.

> After a joyful reunion with his parents, Jack ran around the house making sure everything was in order. He kissed his sister's head and asked why she didn't talk.

In the middle of that first night home, Madeline suddenly became lethargic and struggled to breathe. Sophie rushed her to the small-town emergency room with a 104-degree fever. When the physician recommended helicopter transport to a large children's hospital 250 miles away, Sophie called Mike, who took Jack to the neighbors and met her at the hospital. After a short helicopter ride, Sophie, Mike and Madeline rushed into the neonatal emergency care unit.

A diagnosis of bacterial meningitis required Madeline to stay in the hospital and receive antibiotic treatments for an uncertain 18 days. Mike and Sophie stayed with her at the hospital, keeping family and friends informed about her precarious condition.

Jack, after having landed at the neighbors' in the middle of the night, spent these weeks transitioning every few days between the homes of various friends and relatives. No one knew when or even if Madeline would return home, which meant there was no long-range plan for Jack's care. Sometimes he had his special blanket and teddy bear, sometimes his comfort objects got lost in the shuffle. Jack heard the worry in the adults' voices, especially when they spoke to his parents on the phone. When Jack "spoke" to his parents on the phone, he mostly just listened to his parents' reassurances and praise for being "a big boy."

Once home, Mike, who had missed four weeks of work, went back full-time. He tried to help Sophie with evening childcare but both children only wanted Sophie. If Sophie left the room, Jack screamed and ran to find her.

Sophie tried to balance the needs of both children but found Jack to be the hardest to please. He'd go from pretending he was a baby—refusing to talk, wanting to be carried and spitting out food—to ricocheting around the house. His recent potty learning faded and he had several accidents a day. To conserve her limited energy, Sophie put Jack back in diapers. She worried that he wouldn't be able to start preschool the next month as planned, but sleep-deprivation and Madeline were her biggest concerns. She just needed Jack to be "a big boy." Sophie's mother tried to help out, but Jack refused to leave Sophie's side.

At a follow-up appointment for the baby, Jack ran around the room in circles, stopping each time he passed his mother, to ask in a robotic fashion, "Mommy sit down?" He paused to inspect the fish tank. An older girl ordered Jack not to tap on the glass. Jack responded by hitting the tank with his open hand and running around the room again.

Over the next few months, Jack's behavior became aggressive. When he would have a neighborhood friend over to play, the friend usually would leave because Jack was hitting or spitting. Sophie used time-outs, spankings and threats that she would call his dad to come home from work if Jack's behavior did not improve. Sophie worried about the safety of the baby and would not let the baby or Jack out of her sight.

When Jack was 3, he started preschool but Sophie was called nearly every day to pick him up early. Eventually, the school suggested that the family find a different school that could better meet Jack's needs.

Jack's parents shared this story with me when Jack was 5. He had been kicked out of two childcare centers for disruptive behavior and was now being evaluated by the school district for placement in a special kindergarten for children with emotional problems. The family links the separation at the time of his sister's birth to when Jack's development took a significant turn for the worst.

If I had a magic wand and could retell Jack's story with a different middle and ending, it would go like this:

> Jack ran around the room in circles, stopping each time he passed his mother, to ask in a robotic fashion, "Mommy sit down?" He paused to inspect the fish tank. An older girl ordered Jack not to tap on the glass. Jack responded by hitting the tank with his open hand and again running around the room.
>
> Four weeks later, at a follow-up appointment for the baby, a nurse explained, "Often, when there has been an unexpected change in the family, like your baby's illness, our other children let us know through their behaviors that they, too, are worried or have been impacted. We have a screening tool that you can complete to see if Jack is experiencing anything unusual or to see if he might need some additional support to understand the family changes."
>
> The nurse relayed to the physician her observations of Jack's uncharacteristic behavior, along with the results of the social-emotional screening tool, which measured the significant level of Sophie's and Mike's concerns about him.
>
> While Jack appeared to be physically on-target, the data gathered before and during the examination suggested to the physician that Jack's mom was seeing difficulties in his emotional development. The elevated score on the screening measure suggested that Jack and his parents might benefit from visiting with an expert in early childhood mental health; the pediatrician gave Sophie referral information.

From a clinical point of view, Jack's case is relatively simple. The diagnosis is Adjustment Disorder, which requires a recent stressful event (prolonged separation from his parents) with disturbances in behavior and affect within one month of the event that lasts longer than two weeks. The treatment phase would be brief, most likely a couple of sessions. The first session would be with mom and dad to talk about the unexpected change of events for them and how those events might have impacted Jack. At this session, there might be easy suggestions, such as finding a babysitter for an hour in the afternoon to watch after the critically ill baby while Sophie dedicates special time with Jack. The therapist would discuss Jack's need to be reassured by being held or by getting over-exaggerated hellos and goodbyes, with the prediction that a 2½-year-old boy won't want to be held all the time once he figures out that his parents are not unexpectedly going away again.

A session with the parents and Jack would allow the therapist to help the family explore the issues together, perhaps using play, drawing and other age-appropriate methods. There might be a follow-up session when Jack starts preschool, a time when worries about separation might again resurface and having some expert guidance in setting this next developmental can be helpful.

Imagine this family's positive perception of mental health treatment when they experience an appropriate intervention at the time when the symptoms first emerge, rather than years later when the problems are deeply entrenched and more difficult to change. The more matter-of-factly we communicate with colleagues and parents about the presence of, diagnoses and effective, non-threatening treatment of mental illness in young children, the less power we give that childhood diagnosis to shape a child's emotional or academic destiny.

We practitioners can no longer claim that young children are unaffected by the world around them, will not notice adversity or trauma or will simply "outgrow" their troubles. Jack's story underscores these founding principles. With an estimated 26 percent of American adults suffering in any given year with a diagnosable mental health disorder, we should all be rallying for prevention, early identification and early intervention services (Kessler, Chiu, Demler & Waters, 2005). Remember, we treat ear infections because untreated ear infections increase the likelihood of hearing loss. So why don't we treat mental health disorders in young children?

Fortunately for us and for the children we serve, there is now a growing body of knowledge and clinical techniques available to us that we know can alleviate the suffering of infants, young children and their families (National Scientific Council on the Developing Child, 2008; Zeanah & Zeanah, 2001). Implementing preventive and intervention strategies right now will help restore typical development. Most relevant to early childhood, clinicians and researchers are focused on providing intervention at the earliest point of time to avoid later adverse outcomes.

Diagnostic System for Children under 5

To be able to reliably understand mental health disorders in very young children, to describe the course of the problems within the context of development and to prescribe appropriate treatments, it is essential that clinicians and researchers have systematic criteria for classifying mental health symptoms and developmental disorders. For the adult, adolescent and school-age child, clinicians rely on the traditional tools of the trade: the Diagnostic and Statistical Manual (DSM) or International Classification of Disorders (ICD-10). DSM just received a significant—and thought by many to be overdue—update. However, within the DSM system, few of the criteria and diagnostic classifications are appropriate for very young children, particularly infants, toddlers and preschoolers. Additionally, the method for classifying disorders does not reflect the ways in which infants and young children process, organize and manifest deviant social and emotional development, which is strikingly different from older children and adults. As a result, our research-based knowledge of mental health problems and treatments is negligible for children under the age of 5.

To address the specific needs of clinicians serving very young children and to bring a research-based and systematic approach to assessing mental health symptoms, The Diagnostic Classification of Mental Health and Developmental Disorders of Infancy and Early Child hood (ZERO TO THREE, 1994) and the revised version, DC0-3 Revised Edition [DC0-3R] (ZERO TO THREE, 2005) were developed. Researchers and clinicians need a developmentally appropriate, evidenced-based tool for the systematic identification, assessment and diagnosis of mental health and developmental disabilities in children through age 5. The DC0-3R is based on a complex understanding of early development that provides a bottom-up developmental approach rather than the top-down approach required when using the DSM and ICD systems.

DC0-3R is developed on the tenets that the first few years of life are a time of rapid growth and development, which take place within the context of intimate relationships informed by parental, cultural and community experiences, expectations, and capacities. Assessment and diagnostic protocols for older children and adults do not capture the nuances of early development and the critical role played by primary caregivers in both the development of symptoms and the recovery process. Understanding infant and toddler development requires the clinician to assess the dynamic interaction of unfolding biological potential and an ever-evolving environmental context. Observations of infants, infant-caregiver interaction patterns, temperament, regulatory patterns and individual differences are all key contributors to the assessment process.

Leaving Sophia at childcare has become more and more difficult for Camilla. Sophia has always been shy and slow to warm up in new situations. But after moving into the preschool classroom three months ago, things have progressively gotten worse. At first the teachers reassured Camilla that it was okay for her to leave, even through Sophia would cry for at least 30 minutes. But Sophia still sobs uncontrollably when her mother leaves her and now is resisting going to childcare. Before getting to school, Camilla has had to dress Sophia, carry her to the car and then carry her into the school because Sophia goes completely limp as soon as her mom mentions that it is time to go.

While Sophia tells her mom about the other children in her childcare class, particularly if they get in trouble, the teachers report that she doesn't have friends. Now, the teacher calls Camilla every few days to pick up Sophia early because she is hitting other children and refusing to do what the other children are doing. At naptime, her crying reappears and is some times so intense that she begins to choke or gag. Because Sophia's distress is disrupting the other children in the room and the teachers can't seem to help her, the director has talked with Camilla about finding a school that might better suit Sophia's needs.

At home, things aren't much better. Sophia won't leave Camilla's side. She follows her around everywhere. Camilla has to keep the bathroom door open and shower while Sophia sits outside on the bathroom floor. Bedtime is miserable and frequently ends with Sophia sleeping in mom's bed. Since Sophia is a light sleeper, Camilla has difficulty leaving the bed to watch television in the living room or finish cleaning the evening's dishes.

Sophia's grandmother does not like being left alone at home with Sophia because of her endless crying for her mother. Sophia will sit by the window or door for over an hour waiting for her mother. Sophia's grandmother despairs that there is nothing she can do to get her granddaughter to stop crying for her mother.

Camilla takes Sophia to her 3-year-old well-child visit. She is hoping that she can talk with the pediatrician about getting medication to help Sophia sleep and to provide some relief for the entire family. The nurse hands her two questionnaires about her child's development to complete before she sees the doctor: one regarding general development and the other on social and emotional development. Good, Camilla thinks, this gives her a chance to let Dr. Needlewoman know what a hard time she is having with Sophia. After completing both forms, she and Sophia wait to be called into the physician's office. In the meantime, the nurse scores the screening forms.

The results indicate that Camilla sees her daughter's general development as on target. However, the score on the social and emotional screening measure indicates that Sophia is experiencing difficulties beyond what would be expected of a typical 36-month-old. With this information gathered before the visit, Dr. Needlewoman will spend a few extra minutes learning more about Sophia's current experience and, if indicated, offer a referral to the behavioral clinic newly established within the pediatric practice. She agrees to bring Sophia for a mental health evaluation to help identify the needed strategies to help Sophia find success at home and at school.

Establishing trust and collaboration with parents and other adults, no matter their own challenges, is essential to the diagnostic process and to the treatment of very young children's emotional disorders. Parents are indispensable partners for obtaining complete and accurate information about family history and current circumstances, as well as in helping find successful treatment strategies. Having the mental health evaluation within the pediatric clinic extends the partnership trust of the family.

To assess the psychological functioning of a young child in the context of the child's family, culture and community, the diagnostic process will typically take place over three to five visits, usually scheduled over a period of several weeks. With the advantage of multiple sessions, the clinician has the opportunity to gather comprehensive information through interviews with the parents and other significant caregivers, observations in both formal and informal settings and data collection through standardized assessments. The evaluation is multidisciplinary and includes medical, psychological and language evaluations.

Using the structured decision-making tree encourages clinicians to consider conditions that would not traditionally be considered part of "psychopathology" but that do occur in young children and create immediate problems and subsequent risks for them. For example, young children who have difficulty with regulation (they may persistently over- or under-react to touch, temperature, light and other such stimuli), often experience difficulties in forming relationships, regulating emotions and learning. Therefore, regulatory disorders are included, as well as sleep behavior disorders and eating behavior disorders. Similarly, the impact of experiences with trauma, grief and loss are considered in the diagnostic profile. In addition, the essential role of relationships that structure the lives of children is given ample consideration, thoroughly contextualizing the diagnostic process.

Sophia is experiencing overwhelming and excessive anxiety about being separated from her mother. Teachers and family members cannot console her when her mother is not in her presence and she is now refusing to go to school. Her difficulties with sleep and her need to have her mom constantly by her side are excessive and are interfering with her developing age-appropriate social and emotional capacities. The primary diagnosis is Separation Anxiety Disorder.

Sophia and Camilla's relationship is consumed and overwrought with worries and anxiety. During the formal testing situation, Sophia left the examiner's table to go to mom, who was seated behind her, to ask if she was "right" or if she was "good." Camilla also fretted that she desperately wanted a break from being with Sophia but would worry about her when she was away. Clearly, they both wanted to do their best, but their strengths were being overshadowed by anxiety, tension and over-reaction to ordinary situations.

The assessments documented that while Sophia's cognitive development was on track, her ability to follow-directions and to understand language was limited for a child of her age. She had a vocabulary of a typical 3-year-old but her receptive language was more like that of a younger child. At times, in high language environments, like at school or in larger social gatherings, Sophia couldn't always process all of the information, increasing her feelings of anxiety. Camilla, without previously knowing about the receptive language delay, was naturally quiet, reinterpreting conversations for Sophia by repeating or simplifying what others would say to her.

This family was encountering a great deal of stress. Camilla's husband was on his second military deployment. His first deployment was when Sophia was 9 months old and the second began a few months after her second birthday. For the second deployment, the family decided to move out of their house and Sophia and Camilla went to live with Camilla's mother in a small town in a neighboring state.

Overall, Sophia's emotional capacities were not age-appropriate. When with her mother, Sophia was better able to attend to academic tasks, express her thoughts and solve problems. These capacities were diminished significantly when she worked with someone unfamiliar, like the evaluator, or when her mother was not present, for example, when she was at school. She required a tremendous level of support to stay focused on tasks, to manage her feelings, to tell others what she thought and to solve problems. Rather than be intrigued by new experiences or eager to learn something new, Sophie froze and withdrew.

The treatment goals focused on:

- Restoring age-appropriate attention and regulation across settings.
- Engaging in reciprocal and rewarding interactions with her mother, grandmother, teacher and peers, building towards security in her primary relationships.
- Working with Dad and the family to build connections with Sophia and to help with reintegration when his deployment is over.
- Improving Sophia's receptive language skills while making adults aware of her need for support.
- Providing opportunities for Sophia to build the play skills necessary to express her thoughts and feelings.

The use of DC0–3R diagnoses is helpful in breaking down the stigma around mental health and mental health treatment because they provide the formal structure which frames the concerns expressed by parents and other caregivers about their young children. Diagnosis is not a process of making an arbitrary assumption or picking a diagnosis from a list of possible labels, but instead requires consideration of developmental or mental health difficulty for which structured intervention may be needed.

Thanks to new early childhood development research and better tools and training in the diagnosis and treatment of mental illness in adults and older children, we now know that a young child's diagnosis likewise defines a specific barrier to healthy development. Research programs are both using and informing the field by applying standardized identification and treatment approaches with young children and their families, further improving the validity and reliability of assessing mental health symptoms and successfully treating disorders. By engaging a developmental perspective, we affirm that a child is constantly developing and that early experiences do shape her social and academic trajectory and future prospects.

"Empowers ordinary people to be more effective in caring the health for others in their community, in doing so, become better guardians of their own health."

Vikram Patel, PhD

Mental Health and Early Childhood Settings

Baby's Space is a community-based example of the integration of mental health practices into early childhood settings. Early childhood settings, and particularly childcare, interact on a daily basis with young children and families. At Baby's Space, because we don't provide transportation, we see mom or dad or grandma twice a day, every day. Our multi-service approach allows us to interact with the entire family system. We know, in real time, when there has been a shooting in the neighborhood or if a mom has been kicked out of the grandmother's home.

We also pay close attention to the baby's experience and perspective. "How does the baby see ___?" is a familiar question to teachers and parents alike. We ask everyone to pay attention to what the baby is telling us, particularly with regard to emotional readiness and engagement in learning.

> Wheeled in aboard her navy and white pinstriped stroller, 11-month-old Tamara enters the childcare room. Her black, curly hair frames wide, dark eyes. She is a sturdy child, sitting expressionless and motionless in her stroller. Although this is only the second day of childcare for Tamara, her father, Anthony, pays no attention to the child as they enter the room.
>
> Anthony, a tall 19-year-old with shoulder-length hair pulled into a ponytail, abandons the stroller halfway across the classroom floor, leaving Tamara seated in it. He walks directly to the teacher's desk, where he finds the parent sign-in sheet and completes the necessary paperwork.

Neither looking at nor talking to Tamara or the teachers, Anthony turns and walks out of the classroom, leaving his baby in an unfamiliar setting with adults she barely knows.

Tamara remains seated in the stroller, seemingly without reacting to what has just happened. Her face is unreadable. She shows no sign that she noticed her dad leaving or that she is now aware of having been deposited in this unfamiliar setting. She makes no attempt to communicate with the teachers or children surrounding her. She gives no hint of wanting to depart from her perch. Silently and without moving a limb, she continues to sit in the stroller, apparently waiting for someone else to make the next move.

A teacher, being careful not to frighten the child, slowly approaches Tamara, holding her hands out in a gesture of lifting her from her seat. The teacher waits before touching her to give Tamara the opportunity to signal that she is agreeable to the teacher carrying her from the stroller. Tamara gives no response. She only stares vacantly at the toys lying on the floor in front of her.

Gently, the teacher places her hands under Tamara's arms and picks her up. Like clay that can be formed into any shape, Tamara provides the teacher with neither assistance nor resistance as she is moved from the stroller to the floor. Making slow and reassuring movements, the sensitive and empathic teacher places a few brightly colored, age-appropriate toys within Tamara's reach and then sits nearby. Tamara maintains the position in which she had been placed and remains outwardly indifferent to the teachers, children and toys that surround her.

In the days that follow, despite the teachers' best attempts to engage Tamara, a consistent pattern of disengagement and unresponsiveness continues to pervade all her interactions. During the nine hours that Tamara spends at the childcare center each day, the staff observes that she seems content to sit wherever she is placed, play with whatever toys are within reach and feed herself from a bottle. She rarely demands attention from the staff, who are aware that if they don't make specific plans to interact and care for Tamara, she easily could be ignored and forgotten in the normal noise and commotion of an infant childcare room.

Tamara's indifference and passivity might, in another childcare center, result in her teachers seeing her as "an easy baby." Since she shows no sign of distress as she is easily passed from teacher to teacher, teachers may describe her behavior with positive regard: "It's like she has always been here." By showing no preference for who cares for her, appearing content to play by herself and rarely crying except when she has an urgent need, Tamara demonstrates that in her 11 months of life, she has come to have minimal expectations of those most intimately involved in her life.

When this sort of behavior becomes what is expected of a particular child, caregivers may fail to see and address the underlying significance of this indifference to interaction, the causes and consequences of which may remain unacknowledged until the child reaches her toddler or preschool years. Unfortunately, children like Tamara usually aren't identified until years later, when the inconspicuous infant becomes an aggressive, unfeeling and unruly preschooler. For some children, the development of empathy, compassion and frustration-tolerance is thwarted by a lack of sensitive and consistent responses from her primary caregivers. The number of children expelled from preschool for behavioral problems is alarmingly high.

Think for a moment about Tamara's path: How would she learn to feel concern for others if no one in her early life ever demonstrated to her that she was uniquely important and that she could reliably count on the adults in her life to help her confront daily challenges? Through careful observation, we can see that early on, she learned that her needs and individual desires were unimportant, which in turn made it impossible for her to show empathy, compassion and understanding towards others. In the future, when she wants a toy that another child has, she will get it—and she will do so without regard for the things or people in her path.

> A couple of days later, the teacher greets Tamara and her mom, Tania, as they enter the classroom. She tells both of them how glad she is to see them. After Tania signs in her daughter, the teacher places Tamara's hand in hers and waves to mom while using a sing-song voice: "Bye mom. See you at the end of the day." While the teacher is smiling and looking at Tania, Tamara's head and eyes are turned the opposite direction. Seeing her daughter in the arms of the teacher with eyes turned away, as if defending herself, Tania replies, "She doesn't care about me."

While difficult to acknowledge and knowing that the underlying reasons are significant, Tamara's mom is reading her cues correctly. Tamara is telling the world what, after 11 months, she has learned to expect from others—nothing. When dad left without saying goodbye or mom remarks about her unimportance, they are each telling what they expected from Tamara—nothing. Think of the qualities of the dance between parent and child. The overwhelming characteristic is disengagement with little if any typical development supported by either partner.

Baby's Space provides research-based, neighborhood-centered, culturally relevant services. It practices what every baby already knows: that loving, consistent relationships; basic food and shelter; a safe haven in crisis; and protection from toxic substances, stress and violence help children learn, thrive and contribute. Baby's Space increases children's well-being by helping their families build protective such factors as parent-child relationships, understanding of child development, social connections, stress management and basic needs. Baby's Space's neighborhood-based family services include home-visits, monthly family events and field trips, family advocacy and weekly parent education activities in groups and in one-on-one settings, including prenatal support and doula services.

Baby's Space also provides daily opportunities in a group setting for children to engage in relationships, manage their emotions and learn. Children and families who have experienced trauma or who are physically or emotionally vulnerable receive individualized mental health services within a trusted environment that serves as a point of intervention and safety for children at risk for or involved in child protective services.

With an emphasis on supporting social and emotional development, the teachers, family facilitator, director and mental health provider were ardent observers of both the parents' and child's behaviors and interactions. They understood the significance of early relationships in the formation of the child's sense of self and in affecting the child's abilities to manage emotions, to develop close interpersonal relationships, and to learn by actively exploring the environment. In meeting with the parents, the parents discussed their concerns that Tamara was "slow." Agreeing to partner with the staff to discover how best to help Tamara succeed, the parents met with the mental health provider and family facilitator to complete assessment measures and further discuss their worries about Tamara.

At the same time, the lead classroom teacher was assigned to be Tamara's special teacher, greeting her, changing her diaper, putting her down for nap, paying close attention so that Tamara could develop a one-to-one relationship at the center. The teacher was prepared to respond to any small cue or signal given by Tamara. Initially, Tamara seemed most comfortable taking her bottle on the floor by herself. In response, the teacher sat next to Tamara as she fed herself a bottle, to begin to allow Tamara to connect eating with a person. While it seems like it might be better for the teacher to hold Tamara while she had her bottle, the teacher recognized that the experience would be too different from her customary feeding.

Through the assessment process, the staff discovered that Anthony and Tania were having significant conflicts at home. When asked about Tamara's response to their fights, Anthony said he didn't think Tamara noticed but Tania remembered that sometimes she crawled into the basket under the stroller. With this information, the staff was better able to understand the development of the disengaged patterns. The family facilitator was able to connect the couple with a domestic abuse support center while continuing to work with them to secure stable work and meet basic needs.

For Tamara, shutting down was a good strategy for not getting hurt or in the way of significant conflict but it is a terrible developmental strategy. Her emotional experience was over-regulated, she had no interest or attention in her surroundings or desire for learning. Two-way communication and interests in maintaining relationships were severely limited. At 1 month old, she should display some problem-solving abilities but because her motivation for exploration and engagement were so poor, she rarely encountered problems to solve.

This constellation of behaviors and strategies resulted in Tamara being a rather uninteresting and unrewarding child to parent. When Tania commented that "she doesn't care about me," rather than countering her negative interpretation, the family facilitator understands the significance of her point of view. Even the most competent mothers contend with powerful moments of uncertainty, discontent and often rejection of the maternal role and relationship with their babies. Because of the Baby's Space focus and training on mental health, the family facilitator was aware of the typical range of maternal woes and that the more a mother distances herself from her child, the easier it becomes for parents to make choices that are not in the best interest of their child. As the mother recognizes a family facilitator's willingness to accept all of her feelings—both positive and negative—she will experience tremendous relief when she realizes that we have the ability to help her discuss and manage her conflicting and intense hopes, fears and worries.

The teachers and family facilitator were confident that by working together, they could offer to baby and parents a sensitive, responsive and consistent experience, while at the same time boosting the parents' support and engagement, which in turn would provide a redirection in the child's and family's developmental course. The teacher and family facilitator focused on nurturing the developing relationship between parent and child in an effort to get it back on track towards security and responsiveness. The interventions included consistent relationship-based interactions with Tamara in the classroom, and with the parents through home-visiting and individual support.

Following eight weeks at Baby's Space, in which a specific teacher was assigned the task of recognizing and meeting Tamara's needs while a family facilitator was made available to her parents, we began to see results.

Holding the hand of Tamara, who is seated comfortably on her lap, the teacher attempts to engage the child in the familiar good-bye ritual. "Good-bye Mom. See you at the end of the day. Love you," recites the teacher in her sing-song voice. As on each of the previous mornings, Tamara is not looking towards her mom, but rather at the book in her hand. Tania leaves the childcare room without any acknowledgement from her daughter that she has noticed her mother's departure.

On this morning, however, instead of sitting indifferently in the teacher's lap until directed to the next activity, Tamara rises on her own. Following the path her mother has just taken, she retraces her mother's steps, slowly walking towards the door leading to the hallway. Once at the door, she presses her hands on the door and looks through the window. She stands stock-still for several minutes; her sensitive teacher allows her to make the next move. Turning around, Tamara takes a few steps and falls to the floor. Sobs emerge. Finally, the feelings of separation and loss, so long suppressed, are emerging. With a silent cheer of success, the teacher sits next to Tamara and allows her to crawl into her lap for comfort.

Appreciating the small victory in the development of the relationship between this mother and child, the teacher was aware of the powerful change taking place for the dyad. The teacher's observations were multi-layered and rich in interpretation. Not only did she recognize Tamara's need for comfort and reassurance, she knew the significance of Tamara's delay in reacting to her mother's departure. While still not confident enough to express her feelings of longing and connection directly to her mother, Tamara was rewriting her script by allowing for these feelings to emerge within the safety and predictability of the intervention program. Furthermore, once her needs for basic safety were met and her teacher had repeatedly enforced her ability and willingness to respond to her, Tamara's behaviors in the classroom became more responsive, interactive, and consistent.

Over time, Tamara's responses to interactions made it easier for her to establish secure and trusting relationships with adults, finally allowing herself to exhibit those characteristics and behaviors that favored a secure attachment relationship with those closest to her.

The staff, equipped with keen observation skills and an understanding of the story as told by both Tamara and Tania, knew that Tamara had noticed her mother's departures all along. The staff's job was to allow Tamara to feel that her environment and her relationships with adults were safe enough for her to show her emotional connection to her mother and to her own experiences. As Tamara learned to signal more directly her needs for attention, affection and interaction, she became more enjoyable to care for, which, in turn, allowed her parents to experience success and fulfillment in caring for her.

Changes were also happening in the home. Anthony and Tania decided not to live together and Anthony moved into his parent's home. Tania re-enrolled in the GED program that she had been attending prior to Tamara's birth. Four months after beginning in the program, Tania holds Tamara's hand as they enter the classroom.

Hand-in-hand they cross the room towards the place where the parent check-in sheet is located, greeting the teachers with smiles and warm hellos. While Tania marks the sheet, she chats with the teacher about her job-hunting efforts. Tamara heads to the book corner and returns to her mom with a book in her hands. Tugging on her mom's pants leg, Tamara holds up the book to Tania. In response, Tania glances towards her daughter, pats the black curls on the top of her head and then lowers herself so that she is eye-level with her daughter. Leaning against her mother, Tamara begins to turn the pages of the book as her mom labels the objects on the page.

After finishing the book, Tania tells Tamara that she needs to leave. Tamara and the teacher follow mom to the door. Tania again kneels down to her daughter. Tania and Tamara give each other three kisses good-bye. As Tania nears the door to leave, Tamara holds her hands up towards the teacher indicating that she would like to be held by the teacher.

Working with teachers and a family facilitator who could recognize and embrace the complexity of the individual experiences, emotions and interactions, Tania and Tamara shifted the odds of Tamara successfully developing a secure-base for her future relationships and accomplishments heavily in the child's favor. The infant who entered childcare amidst concerns that her development was off track emerges as one of the brightest and most engaged preschoolers in the center.

As remarkable as Tamara's case may seem, her triumph over what seemed a bleak situation presents further evidence of the strength of resiliency of young children and the effectiveness of early intervention programs that address both the behaviors and interactions of the parents and child. Tamara's strengths were her young age at the time she entered Baby's Space, designed to be a prevention-intervention program for young children at risk because of the complications of poverty, community and domestic violence and historic trauma. Biological wiring, present in very young children, is set up to seek a responsive, predictable and consistent relationship with at least one adult. In fact, many characteristics that enhance affirmative interactions between a baby and his primary caregiver are wired-in for most children and, if hidden, sometimes just need consistent and responsive coaxing to re-emerge.

Tamara and Tania allow us to see how creating a base of security for a child can be influenced by a variety of features and experiences brought into the relationship not only by the parent but also by the child, and by the environment that supports the family as a whole. One of the key components of this dyad's success was Tania's and Tamara's abilities to transform their interactions from flat and indifferent to engaged and responsive. Helping the child and mother rewrite their expectations and interactions with others benefits the burgeoning security of her relationship with her mother.

Equal care for the parents

Coinciding with the positive interactions shared by the dyad, Tania was able, with the support of the program staff, to seek assistance for the domestic violence in her life. Finally able to protect herself, she became a powerful ally for her daughter as well. The strong and meaningful relationships the program staff developed with both mother and daughter helped strengthen their confidence in themselves and foster a sense of esteem and importance.

A key component of success for Tamara and Tania was the ability of the staff to both recognize and support the disconnection between mother and child. While most mothers experience maternal ambivalence in varying degrees, few providers feel prepared to discuss these intense and contradictory feelings directly with mothers. As a result, many providers fail to take advantage of the office visit as a valuable opportunity to complete in-depth parenting evaluations, to hear and respond to a mother's despair or to unearth and explore her long-buried frustrations with the demands of parenthood.

The helping professional often tries to counter a negative comment with a positive one, concede the mother's rejection of her newborn as transient or due to hormonal changes or dismiss concerns of maternal harshness. After all, it is uncomfortable to think of a mother as anything but instinctively nurturing and unconditionally loving.

Yet it is precisely in understanding and accepting the experience of maternal ambivalence as an experience common to many mothers that providers will become willing and able to help their parents deal with its effects. By increasing one's awareness of the typical range of maternal ambivalence and one's knowledge of strategies that can assist a parent in acknowledging and managing negative feelings, the provider becomes a powerful ally in supporting the mother-child relationship.

While maternal ambivalence is typical, particularly under stressful circumstances, it is essential that providers feel prepared to distinguish between the conditions which allow a mother to tolerate her ambivalent feelings without comprising her capacity to care for her child, and those conditions which foster the mother's neglect and maltreatment of her baby. For example, when the mother has inadequate support, little knowledge of child development and limited personal resources, the task of overcoming and understanding her ambivalence is far more complicated and worrisome.

Personal challenges of substance abuse, untreated depression, other mental illness, teenage pregnancy and domestic violence can compromise the mother's ability to make choices that are in the best interest of her baby. In these situations, unaddressed feelings of maternal ambivalence can undermine or distort a mother's hopes and expectations for her relationship with her child. Without support or assistance, she is left in a position to direct these powerful negative feelings towards her baby, at times resulting in serious and life-threatening consequences.

When extreme ambivalence goes unchecked, the overt or covert maltreatment of the baby appears to the mother as an acceptable way of dealing with these deeply disturbing emotions. In such situations a provider must be prepared to address not only the immediate neglect or maltreatment of a child, but also the source and extent of the mother's ambivalence. In order to do so, providers must have access to effective strategies for helping mothers manage the tremendous tasks of parenthood, particularly when the mother struggles in regulating her emotions and managing her own vulnerabilities.

Putting the baby's point-of-view at the center of full-service childhood development programming, Baby's Space engenders successful children, healthier families, and transforms neighborhoods of poverty. Our vision is, with the baby-centered approach, to graduate children (and families) who are healthy, compassionate, well adjusted, prepared and educated, to become contributors to thriving neighborhoods.

7

"Children's mental health depends on healthy families
and strong communities. We must start early on."
T. Berry Brazelton

COMMUNITY READINESS

The value of protecting and intervening early in the lives of young children and families clearly leads to better outcomes. But the "typical" category isn't a one-size-fits-all. Infants, young children and parents can have vastly different approaches to new situations, people and activities. Some children begin their journeys with wonderful qualities that make them relatively "user-friendly": emotional flexibility, ease with lower-energy activities like reading or outgoing interests in people. Parenting these babies is easier. Other babies have digestive difficulties, immature nervous systems or heightened reactions to sounds or touch that require more sensitive caregiving. And, for a few children, the path begins by negotiating developmental challenges, disruptions in caregivers or other stressful events. Parents also bring their own successes and challenges in fulfilling their critical roles as nurtures, protectors and teachers.

We, as community members, educators, health providers and policymakers, need to ensure that each baby is on a path to success by taking the baby's point of view and asking, "how is the baby?"

"He's easygoing until he wants something."
Parent

READY ADULTS

As caring adults, there are many things we can do to safeguard a baby's development. Providing a safe environment for play and exploration in which a small team of consistent and caring adults attends to the baby's needs is our first priority. Babbling, talking and reading to the baby provides a rich language environment that supports the baby's growing vocabulary and interest in the world. Our job as adults is to help manage experiences the baby is too young to handle alone. Our being a reassuring presence allows the infant to communicate more clearly, the toddler to learn to sleep soundly and the preschooler to manage the frustrations of sharing.

We want all the members of the baby's team—mom, dad, grandma and teacher—to understand the importance of their caregiving relationship in the baby's long-range success. When adults embrace the critical nature of their jobs, they set the stage for the child's future expectations and success in school and relationships. A child does best when the team of adults sends the same message: "You, baby, matter." When the baby's team provides consistent, nurturing and responsive interactions, the child develops confidence in others, self-confidence and the empathy and compassion to care for others.

To be effective partners in a child's positive development, we must dedicate ourselves to being keen observers of that child's feelings and experiences. A baby can't tell us in words what she needs, but we can observe her face, body and behavior for that information. Labeling her experiences helps reinforce what we see and know about the baby and helps her develop understanding and meaning of internal experiences: "You are excited." "You are so mad!" When we watch how a baby handles transitions, new situations or a favorite toy, we customize our approach to mirror the best interests of the baby. By developing the understanding that the baby's behaviors have meaning, we begin to see from the baby's point of view, not just our own.

"Biting is not okay but we have to figure out what he is trying to tell us."
Teacher

If we switch our vantage point and look at the child's experiences from the child's view—as well as from our adult view—we are more prepared to help the baby develop essential capacities for emotional and social success. Each interaction helps a baby fortify the ability to regulate both internal and external experiences, learn to communicate effectively and engage in relationships.

A toddler needs adults to promote these foundational and growing abilities. When we embrace teaching in everyday moments, we see how a toddler can learn to effectively communicate "me cookie" and manage the internal reaction to limit setting, "one cookie, not two." These skills set the foundation for being able to wait for a turn, listen to the teacher at circle time and get along with other children on the playground. It is through everyday interactions that a child builds, practices and rehearses emotional know-hows for success.

Our other critical job as caring adults is to buffer, protect and pay attention to sudden changes in behavior, interactions with others, life events or sensitivities, as experienced by the child. We now understand that not all children come with the same fortitude or internal capacities. The child's care team must understand how this particular baby experiences the world, both internally and externally. Stressful or traumatic events require the presence of a protective adult who is able to think in the best interest of the child at the time of an adverse event or situation.

Parent education and support

Consistency, predictability and sensitivity are the crown jewels of parenting. Whether responding to a cry, establishing a bedtime routine, limiting cookies or managing a tantrum, caregivers must learn the skills to positively and decisively handle the everyday parent-child dilemmas. Finding and practicing effective strategies are essential to positive caregiving experiences and healthy adult-child relationships.

Parents need practical strategies presented in ways that are easy to understand and make sense in the context of their lives and goals.

A young child thrives when the team of adults is dependable, uses the same consistent approach and creates an environment that is harmonious and positive. Sometimes even members of the same have vastly different ideas about parenting. Because the very young child is dependent on the adults around him, he has a heightened sensitivity to disagreement, inconsistent approaches, conflict and hostility. Caregivers who provide the same level of responsiveness, expectations and strategies make it easier for the child to be successful and to learn. After all, the baby directly learns about respect, empathy and trust by experiencing the ways in which the adults around him interact with each other. We must invest in our own communication and in building supportive relationships with each other.

Parents who get support from their family, friends and teachers are better able to garner the resources they need to be predictable and sensitive caregivers and attend to their children's social, emotional and academic needs. Social support helps us build and maintain strategies to manage the daily grind of responsive caregiving. When we surround ourselves with others who embrace the momentous responsibility of raising emotionally health children along and have a realistic understanding of both the joys and challenges of parenting, we are better able to see the child's perspective and experiences as equal to our own.

There are many parenting programs that have been shown to effectively help parents and caregivers successfully navigate methods for encouraging positive behaviors and handling problem behaviors. Making parent education a typical and accessible part of parenting, encourages everyone to develop the skills and resources to support child development, embrace the prominence of quality of the parent-child relationships, receive the social support, the confidence to manage life's ups and downs, and the skills to effectively managing their children's behaviors. I find that specifically learning strategies to help toddlers negotiate their burgeoning independence is an essential stage of parent coaching. The skills needed to manage a 2-year-old's quest for independence with her development limitations are similar proficiencies that parents need later for overseeing homework or negotiating curfews.

The typical woes of parenting can be additionally challenging for parents who as children experienced inconsistencies in adult availability, neglect, became primary caregiver for younger siblings or faced harsh discipline. Our parents may have made mistakes or have been unavailable because of their own issues or unrecognized traumas. While it clearly is not our responsibility for the poor caregiving received, it is our responsibility as parents to choose and implement positive parenting strategies and develop warm and secure relationships with our children. Investing in our abilities in parenting through parent education, coaching and therapy breaks the cycles of maltreatment and helps secure our children's pathways for success.

As part of a caring team of adults, it is critical that we pay attention when mothers and fathers are struggling with their own mental health. Maternal and paternal depressions are treatable with a variety of approaches. It is always heartbreaking to me when a woman tells me of her untreated depression and the way it impacted the relationship with her child. For the sake of the children, the parent-child relationships and the health of the parent, we all need to support appropriate mental health screening and treatment.

"I can walk in and know exactly what goes on with my kids and what to expect! I have also grown up here at Baby's Space myself. I learned how to be a better parent by watching and observing and asking questions. Not ever being afraid to ask even the hard questions!"

Parent

EMBRACING NEIGHBORHOOD CHILDCARE

The landscape for families with young children in the 21st century has changed from that of previous generations. Most infants, toddlers and preschool children are cared for by adults who are not their parents; the majority of mothers are employed outside the home and families living in poverty are no longer subsidized to stay home to raise their children. Many families can count on grandparents or other family members, friends and neighbors to provide care for their young children. These childcare arrangements often help parents feel confident that their children are receiving care most similar to what they experience at home. Moreover, a family member or friend often shares the same cultural values and expectations and allows for more one-to-one attention.

But not all parents have the option of a family member or friend who is available and capable of providing full-time childcare. Sometimes illness, family conflicts or the special needs or temperament of a child can limit the viability of home-based childcare.

Natalie and Jeron were anticipating the upcoming birth of their second child. Both teachers, they looked forward to having the summer to spend with their 16-month-old son Tyrell and the newborn. Anticipating returning to work in September, they evaluated their childcare options. Unfortunately, their sister-in-law, who had been taking care of Tyrell since he was 6 weeks old, and whom he loved, was moving with her family to another state. A home-based provider who took care of another teacher's child had openings for Tyrell and the new baby, and a family friend who was home full-time with her own toddlers offered to watch the two children two days per week without charge. Natalie and Jeron both liked the idea of splitting childcare between the home-based provider and the family friend because it was less expensive than center-based childcare or using full-time, home-based childcare. They saw using the family friend as similar to having their sister-in-law care for the children.

While childcare from family, friends and neighbors can be a great option for many families, life events, changes in family dynamics or characteristics of children and adults may result in numerous changes in childcare arrangements during the first few years of a child's life. Parents look at the realities of cost, convenience, quality and continuity and then worry about whether they are making the right decisions or causing unforeseen harm to their children. As with Natalie and Jeron, cost is an important factor in the choice of childcare arrangements. Nearly 30 percent of children under the age of 5 are in multiple childcare arrangements each week. With expected and unanticipated changes in providers, imagine how many transitions of significant child care providers a child might experience in his first five years.

FROM THE BABY'S POINT OF VIEW

Mom and dad think 20-month-old Tyrell is going through the terrible twos early! He is uncooperative, sleeping poorly and a picky eater. He cries when he is dropped off at childcare and when he is picked up.

From Tyrell's perspective, a lot has changed. He doesn't see his beloved auntie. A new baby appeared who cries a lot. And his mom and dad leave him for long periods of time at the houses of other people. When he wakes up in the morning, he doesn't know whom he will be with, where he will be for the day or what kind of food he will eat.

While the NICHD (2010) found that high-quality center-based childcare increases academic achievement even at third grade, too often parents make childcare decisions for financial reasons that may decrease the likelihood of the engagement of high-quality early childhood providers and programs. A few national childcare chains provide nationally accredited childcare, but these centers are not universally available, particularly not in neighborhoods of high poverty. Because for-profit centers rely primarily on parent payment, access is restricted for families with limited income. The staff at for-profit centers may not reflect the cultural or community values of the family, tend to receive low compensation and often have high turnover.

"Baby's Space has always been and always will be home for my kids and me. Especially when I need help. Always keeping the kids number one, always, always and the staff is always dependable. You know that kids will be taken care of. The staff communicate really well. It's awesome!"

Parent

A Local Changemaker

Built on the premise that quality child development services offer a strategic and early intervention point for at-risk children, Baby's Space provides what a baby wants and needs: loving relationships that are warm, sensitive, consistent and responsive. I believe that neighborhood-based nonprofit childcare centers like Baby's Space can equalize the current child development system, providing families with a full spectrum of evidence-based services needed for success: high-quality childcare, parent education and family services. In elevating childcare centers from babysitting while parents are working to sites for integrated child and family education, we help create whole communities that see through the eyes of their children.

Much like the convenience of a superstore, neighborhood-based childcare centers can provide integrated one-stop child development centers in which full-day, full-year child and family services are of equal importance. For example, a mother can bring her child to the childcare and stop to talk with a staff member about her worries about a violent boyfriend, eliminating the inconvenience of visiting another counselor at a different agency. As a local hub of support, consistency and stability for both children and families, the childcare center can be transformational, providing the quality of childcare and parent support that can make a significant difference in children's development.

Located in the family's neighborhood, the childcare center functions in much the same way as neighborhood elementary schools, providing a trusted setting for the care and education of young children that reflects the needs and goals of the surrounding families. Raising awareness of the importance of early experiences and emotional well-being encourages teachers, parents and neighborhood residents to put a high priority on the needs of children and to better understand how their actions and decisions impact infants, toddlers and preschool children. Engaging community-based staff, a neighborhood childcare center further infuses the neighborhood with the baby's perspective.

Plus, nonprofit childcare centers tend to have a do-what-it-takes attitude that can bring the best opportunities directly to families. They tend to invest more in hiring staff from the local community, which helps ensure that community members become the best advocates for children and the program, and that parents, elders and neighbors participate in an ongoing conversation about how best to care for the community's youngest members.

> Cherry brings her 6 month-old, daughter Blossom, into the infant classroom. Greeted by the cheerfulness of Julia, the infant teacher, Cherry recites the maladies of her morning. Julia's positive engagement and warm presence do nothing to thwart Cherry's prediction of the misfortunes for her upcoming day. Perhaps because of her youth and history, the words Cherry uses to talk with her daughter and with the staff are harsh and punctuated with four-letter words. The bib hanging around Blossom's neck sums up Cherry's message to the world: "My Mama's a Bitch."

> Blossom was the result of an unplanned pregnancy. The baby's father is in prison. Cherry's family who believes that she needs to handle her poor choices on her own, has had limited support from her family. She has struggled in school and recently enrolled in a local alternative high school program.

> Led by our home visitor, our team worked to give Cherry messages of support while at the same time helping her see the impact of her language and interactions with her daughter. Through parent groups and casual contact,

Cherry began to see how, regardless of the age of her child, her interactions and words mattered. We were consistent in our interactions and in our belief that Cherry was so much more than the message on her baby's bib, and she began to change.

Feeling the support of the staff, Cherry began participating regularly in home visits, infant/toddler groups and family nights. As a result of these supportive interactions, Cherry began to give Blossom a kiss when she dropped her off each day—and got one in return. Today, Cherry knocks on the door of our family person with a smile and a greeting.

Blossom, now 13 months old, has a robust vocabulary of 11 words and a delightful connection to mom and teachers. At family nights, she and her mom sit together, kissing each other on the cheek. Cherry is in a work-support program and has finished school, and the relationship between Blossom and her mom has, well, blossomed! Most important, Blossom's development has improved each day. Her first two-word sentences were, "kiss mama," and "luff you," because her mom is a good teacher.

While there are many successful and high-quality nonprofit childcare centers, there has not been a model for how an existing neighborhood-based center can operate as a one-stop child development center, implementing evidence-based practices and acting as an agent of community change. From our experiences at Baby's Space and with other organizations throughout the country, we believe that there are three key ingredients: a strong financial system, quality programming and training and director support. Baby's Space has benefited from local organizations and agencies in developing strengths in each of these areas. The high-quality, effective programs that helped us are replicable.

Strong financial system

A finance model, Strong Beginnings, created by Hennepin County in Minnesota, provides an excellent example of a public mechanism for providing both resources and guidelines to ensure quality, full-service programs. Designed to detect and remediate developmental challenges, promote school readiness and engage parents in their child's learning, the majority of children in Strong Beginnings programs were solidly on track for academic success. Ninety percent of the children enrolled in the program received subsidized childcare in which state rates were enhanced by the county program. (Miller, 2005)

Most childcare centers operate with funding from only one or two sources. Braided funding that includes multiple funding sources—public funding, foundation support and individual donors—is essential to ensure continuity and breadth of services. Designed specifically for childcare centers, Children's First Finance developed the Growth Fund Program, which provides comprehensive business development. Enlisting a volunteer board of advisors, Children's First Finance provides support for planning and implementation of customized business improvement plans for nonprofit childcare organizations.

Quality

Ratio matters. Particularly in a group setting, the number of children must be determined by the ability of the adult to provide consistent and nurturing care. Too few adults can require infants and toddlers to behave in ways that are developmentally most challenging: following rules, waiting their turns, and managing their peer relationships.

National accreditation provides one mechanism for ensuring the highest quality standards in environment, curriculum, services and evaluation. Twin Cities United Way is addressing quality by investing to help local childcare centers develop programs that meet and even exceed national accreditation. After participating in the Childcare

Accreditation Program, Baby's Space achieved six out of 10 perfect scores in reaccreditation.

The Classroom Assessment Scoring System (CLASS)™ is a tool developed to assess early childhood teachers' warmth, attentiveness and respect in interactions with children—essential qualities of responsive teaching. The CLASS™ helps teachers and directors focus on the specifics of effective teaching and interactions that promote student learning.

> "He's a brat. No wait, I am at Baby's Space. My son is challenging."
> *Parent*

Training and empowering

Programming from the baby's point of view is as much about the "how" as the "what." Critical decisions about the programs, staffing, space and family services must be checked against the critical question, "How does the baby see it?" Working with children to develop academic skills, like letter and number recognition, caregivers and childcare staff must remember that this academic training serves an essential role in the development of the children's social and emotional skills like focusing attention, emotional regulation, two-way communication and forming and maintaining relationships.

Our work at Baby's Space and with other childcare centers and Head Start organizations in Minnesota has helped us develop a suite of practical products that enhance the abilities of neighborhood-based teachers, home visitors and directors to maintain quality and enhance emotional readiness and school success. Bringing the child's point of view into all efforts, our professionally designed early learning environments and step-by-step resource materials align with early learning standards.

While most childcare staff understand their role in supporting the educational development of children, our vision is to create transformational centers where staff and parents are interested and ready to be more involved in shaping the future of their neighborhoods, ensuring that their children receive the opportunities and have the skills necessary for college and career success. Partnering with Twin Cities RISE!, we have jointly created Personal Empowerment courses for childcare teacher and community-based providers, which allows individuals to make the internal changes necessary to be transformational. We believe that combining the baby's point of view with the belief in one's ability to make the changes necessary for success creates a powerful and sustained model for neighborhood success.

Hubs of Excellence in Neighborhood Childcare

Baby's Space's innovations in design, customer use and messaging of the principles of emotional health are transformational in early learning environments. We do not replicate education created for older children and simply shrink it down. We use the baby's point of view to direct service, training, environmental design, and organizational coaching. Our practical strategies help others' understanding that in order to learn compassion or the ABCs, each child first needs to be treated as special and deserving, and that infants' trauma cannot be ignored. And, rather than building new centers or creating new nonprofit organizations, Baby's Space works to bring university-based ideas to local organizations and school districts that best know their communities.

We envision locally based hubs that support the staff, program directors and program enhancements of neighborhood-based child care centers. Together these neighborhood-based centers are recognized with an overarching brand, join together for coaching and mentorship and collaborate to support strong financial and high-quality programs. In so doing, we can enlist the power of local communities, neighbors and parents to create meaningful change in the emotional readiness and academic success of young children and their families.

"I never thought about how my accident impacted my toddler."
Parent

EARLY AND ACCESSIBLE
MENTAL HEALTH SERVICES

Investing in early childhood development helps us build strong and prosperous neighborhoods and communities. Now is the time to create early and accessible mental health services that benefit the development of young children and their families. Trauma and stress that impacts brain development interrupts the developmental process. Left unrecognized and untreated, children, families and communities face protracted problems and soaring intervention expenses.

The key lies in our abilities to clearly define early childhood social and emotional health and to develop systems for screening, identifying and treating emotional difficulties experienced by young children. In one school system in a rural community, the superintendent maintained that children in his district could not be considered to have mental health problems until seventh grade. When we look at the disruption in school systems, correctional facilities and families that may be caused by older children with problems, it is understandable that adults focus heavily on the most problematic children.

Recognizing Distress in Children

When we are worried about whether a young child's behavior is normal, or if an event has impacted the child's well being, we must be strong advocates for the child's development. When we fail to address the changes in the child's behavior, or assume that the baby or toddler will outgrow it and get on with typical development, we may contribute to the weakening of the child's emotional foundation. We don't ignore it when a child is tugging at the ears and running a low-grade fever because we know that an ear infection can have a long-term—and permanent—affect on hearing. Just as with ear infections, there are ways to screen and assess symptoms of emotional health.

By using valid and reliable emotional health screening measures during times of typical development and at times of concern, we safeguard typical development and can determine when further assessment is needed. Making screening available through your medical clinic, early childhood program or public health service can help caring adults determine if a child is on track—or confirm that the nagging little worries merit a professional evaluation.

New Model for Treatment

Our traditional adult model of clinic-based treatment creates barriers to timely and accessible care for very young children and their families. When parents are referred to mental health specialists outside of their communities, fear of stigmatization and the understandable denial of the child's problem being "that bad" thwart the best efforts of providers. In general mental health clinics, few clinicians see children under the age of 5; as a result, the family may have to wait months for an appointment.

Primary care and early childhood settings offer trusted environments for screening as well as assessment and treatment. If mental health services are embedded in these familiar locations, children and families are more likely to receive timely and effective early assessment and intervention services. Strong partnerships between parents, healthcare providers and childcare centers can enhance the consistency and effectiveness of interventions and respond with agility to improvements or changes in behaviors or life circumstances. Childcare centers with embedded parenting programs also can be part of the treatment and after-care plan, helping ensure continued success for the child and the family.

When parents get timely and effective help with emotional challenges experienced by their young children, it helps build a commitment to supporting and monitoring the emotional readiness and mental health of those children. If parents have successful experiences, they may become more likely to seek services as needed for older children or even themselves. By investing in our youngest children, who clearly need supportive and protective environments for healing and well-being, we may transform our societal understanding of emotional health and importance of early recognition and intervention.

"We must create the culture for the world we want to live in."
Nate Garvis

READY COMMUNITIES

The best way to ensure school success is to support the emotional readiness of very young children and to build networks of support for families. Our actions as leaders, staff, neighbors and parents communicate volumes about the importance of early relationships babies have with their team of caring adults. If we want children to be ready for kindergarten, we must be certain that the environments and systems we create are responsive to the unique developmental needs of not only preschoolers but infants, toddlers and their families.

The everyday happenings experienced by infants and toddlers impact their development. Who takes care of them, where they go for childcare, if they are hospitalized or placed in foster care: all experiences—good and bad—impact the architecture of their brains and their abilities to engage in relationships, manage their emotions and learn. Health development is dependent on a team of consistent, caring and sensitive adults.

Babies are neither resilient nor unbreakable. Early experiences, disruptions in caregivers and trauma can be toxic to the development of young children. For children and families struggling with trauma, unexpected transitions or their own health difficulties, we need accessible screening, assessment and intervention services to safeguard children. For young children, intervention is prevention— early detection and quick and effective treatment minimizes the risk for later and protracted problems.

Policies and programs that value and support the central role of the family in ensuring the baby's emotional health and readiness for school are essential. There are many powerful actions we can take as parents, educators, childcare providers and policymakers:

- Improve preconception and prenatal care for all women in order to reduce long-term health complications and later special education services by:

- Supporting preconception health, including the use of folic acid, of all women in your family and community of childbearing age (U.S. Preventive Services Task Force, 2009).
- Improving access to prenatal health care for all women through health care coverage, public policy and health care campaigns.
- Promoting mental health screening for all pregnant and newly parenting women. Encourage and support treatment for those experiencing symptoms.
- Encouraging substance-free pregnancies—no smoking, no alcohol and no illicit drugs.
- Changing state and federal policies to include birthing support and other innovative approaches to improving pregnancy outcomes and maternal health.

- Establish 21st century approaches to improving the knowledge of child development, commitment to parenting, social support, and resiliency in managing stress for all parents with the goal of building stronger families and communities. Support healthy parenting practices by:
  - Realizing that relationships are the cornerstone of early development, we can commit to being part of a child's team of consistent, sensitive and nurturing adults.
  - Working with policymakers to establish paid family leave including at least 14 weeks universal leave for new mothers, and intermittent leave that supports families with children with special health care needs.
  - Recognizing that becoming a parent is like being a new driver, lots of years of observation but not experience behind the wheel—everyone needs education, skill development and a coach.
  - Creating parent-to-parent support in which similar cultural values create opportunities for learning within a trusting environment.
  - Integrating evidenced-based parenting programs and

promising practices, including school-district family education into neighborhood-based childcare centers.

- Providing intensive and effective parent-child services for families struggling with histories of trauma, maltreatment and at-risk for dysfunctional parenting practices.

- Make available high-quality neighborhood-based child care centers as the epicenter of family and child development. We can create these critically important enriching early childhood settings by:

  - Recognizing that the majority of fathers and mothers are in the workforce and providing affordable, high-quality experiences for infants, toddlers and preschool age children is at the pinnacle of needs for 21st century families and our future economy and well-being.

  - Informing parents and the general public about the value to society of high-quality early experiences, particularly in childcare, to the future development of children and our future workforce and society.

  - Establishing neighborhood-based, high-quality childcare with integrated parenting services to provide proven and effective child and family services.

  - Reframing funding and policies for childcare as essential, high-quality settings of early development rather than parent-employment strategies and provide regulations and funding similar to Early Head Start, Head Start and other national, research-based programs.

  - Designing systems including rating systems and branding of full-service neighborhood-based non-profits child development centers so that parents are aware and able to more easily access quality settings.

  - Providing publically funded full-day kindergarten allows for a full-range of educational and social opportunities for 5-year-old children, better preparing them for elementary success.

- School districts are well positioned to make available high-quality district-based child care centers based on the work schedules of teachers.

- These childcare centers would serve teachers and school district staff, community parents, and teen parents enrolled in high school.
- Rather than budgets based on operations for 52 weeks per year and 11 hours per day, these centers operations would reflect the district schools schedules (38 to 40 weeks) and reduced hours, making high-quality childcare more affordable for parents.
- Consistency and education of the staff, and quality of the center, reflect the district's commitment to school success and emotional readiness of all young children.

- Require health care providers and health insurers to provide developmental and social-emotional screenings as part of routine well-child exams by:
  - Asking primary care providers to screen for emotional and social development using a valid tool.
  - Providing adequate reimbursement for pediatric and family practices to provide child development guidance and family-centered care.
  - Integrating mental health and physical health practices, particularly for very young children and their families.
  - Create new models for accessible and effective mental health services by:
  - Understanding that young children are vulnerable to unexpected events, traumas and separations that can fundamentally change their courses of development.
  - Paying attention to the earliest of experiences of infants, toddlers and preschoolers and recognizing that behaviors have meaning.
  - Recognizing the value of early intervention compared with dealing with more protracted problems in older children and adults.
  - Designing new access points for screening, assessments,

and interventions including primary care practices and child care centers.

- Using evidenced-based and promising practices to help ameliorate psychological suffering of young children and families.

By using the baby's point of view to inform our interactions, programs and policies, we can provide every child in every neighborhood with the chance to develop the emotional tools and academic skills necessary for school success.

NOTE ON THE ORGANIZATIONS IN THIS BOOK

There are best-practice model organizations throughout the United States. Those listed here have contributed to our work at Baby's Space and/or provide excellent examples for model programs that can work towards fostering success in pregnant and parenting families and their young children.

Baby's Space, LLC

As a leader in the early child development field, Terrie Rose saw that children born into communities of high poverty had limited learning opportunities and were at high risk of toxic stress, abuse and neglect—factors that often lead to significant developmental delays, social and emotional difficulties, school failure and dropout. She founded Baby's Space with an environment created—literally—from the ground up, using a baby's perspective. The first facility was in a converted school across the street from an American Indian housing development, a financially challenged community in Minneapolis. Today, Baby's Space provides a full range of educational and support services, including childcare and elementary education.

Baby's Space, LLC offers training, products and consultation to other organizations that are working to support the emotional readiness and academic success of young children and their families. Baby's Space products and training benefit organizations across the county, including childcare centers, Early Head Start and Head Start in urban areas and on reservations. Directors, teachers and caregivers face special challenges as they work with very young children and families, particularly those living with poverty and trauma. Baby's Space curriculum products and consultation support directors, teachers and home visitors in providing effective and engaged services.

The Birthing Project

Founded by Ashoka fellow Kathryn Hall Trujillo, The Birthing Project is dedicated to improving the birth outcomes of women of color. The Sister-Friend Program provides one-on-one support for at-risk pregnant women using a community-based mentor to help navigate the medical system and ensure quality pre- and postnatal healthcare. Community doulas and other programs offer practical and ongoing support to children, mothers and fathers.

Educare

The Ounce of Prevention in Chicago and the Buffett Early Childhood Fund have created a model for combining public and private dollars to create comprehensive early childhood centers serving 150 to 200 children under the age of 6 and their families. Identifying and creating partnerships between anchor philanthropist, Head Start partner, school superintendent and community stakeholders, the team creates an Educare Center built to provide high-quality, effective early childhood and family support programs.

First Children's Finance

First Children's Finance, led by Gerald Cutts, provides business-development assistance and loans to high-quality childcare business serving low- and moderate-income families. Understanding the complexities of running the business of childcare, First Children's Finances bring resources available in other market places to those most in need of financial guidance and support. Through the Growth Fund, FCF enlists a volunteer board of advisors to help nonprofit childcare organizations plan and implement customized business improvement plans.

Fussy Baby Network

The Fussy Baby Network helps parents of fussy babies connect with infant specialists and providers who understand the challenges of infant crying, sleeping and feeding. Parent "warmlines," home visiting programs, parenting groups and specialized clinics provide opportunities for parents to share concerns about their babies' health and development and to receive knowledgeable guidance and support.

HealthConnect One

Community-based doulas provide support to underserved women during pregnancy, birth and the early months of parenting. By training and employing doulas from the same community as their clients, HealthConnect One embraces the power of peer support, helping build healthier birth outcomes and stronger and more responsive neighborhoods.

Mother-Baby Program

Spearheaded by psychiatrist Dr. Helen Kim, the Hennepin County Mother-Baby Program offers a range of mental health services to support mothers, babies and their families. The Mother-Baby Hopeline provides triage and resources to pregnant and parenting mothers. The Day Hospitalization, which opened in 2013, is the fourth in the country to provide customized mental health day treatment to women experiencing the debilitating symptoms of depression and anxiety.

Teachstone

The executive leadership for Teachstone is provide by Dr. Robert Pianta, who is ranked in the top 20 of most influential university-based scholars in the United States. Coming from the same graduate program, we share a commitment to the social and emotional development of young children and a passion to improve the teaching and learning interactions between teachers and children. The CLASS ™ Tool helps educators improve the engagement in classroom environments beginning with toddlers.

Twin Cities RISE!

Founded by Ashoka fellow Steve Rothchild in 1994, Twin Cities RISE! developed a number of job-training strategies to improve the salaries of un- and under-employed adults who come from generational histories of poverty. Personal Empowerment, which helps participants make the internal changes necessary for sustained success, is a signature program of TCR! Baby's Space and TCR! are working together to bring Personal Empowerment to early childhood and family educators and program directors.

TED & TEDx Talks

TED provides opportunities for us to learn and to be inspired. The following talks have informed and transformed our thinking.
- Ann Murphy Paul: *What we learn before we're born.*
- Alexander Tsiaras: *Conception to birth—visualized.*
- Tyrone Hayes & Penelope Jagessar Chaffer: *The toxic baby?*
- Cortney Giffin: *Epigenetics makes you unique.*
- Thomas Insel: *Toward a new understanding of mental illness.*
- Art Rolnick: *Economic case for early childhood development.*
- Peter Benson: *Sparks: How youth thrive*
- Nate Garvis: *Change our culture, change our world.*
- Vikram Patel: *Mental health for all by involving all.*
- Terrie Rose: *From the baby's point of view.*

ABOUT THE AUTHOR

Dr. Terrie Rose is a child psychologist and leader in the field of early childhood and family development. As founder of Baby's Space and Tatanka Academy, an innovative nonprofit based in Minneapolis, Minnesota, that is a full-service child development center for low-come young children and their families, Terrie brings research and best practice to the everyday experience of young children and families living in poverty and trauma. Recognized for her system-changing solution, she is an Ashoka Fellow and received support from Social Venture Partners. Her TEDx Talk, From the Baby's Point of View, inspired this book. Terrie has received awards for her leadership from the National Child Labor Committee, Minnesota Department of Health and the Minnesota Association of Children's Mental Health. Previously, Terrie was the associate director for the Irving B. Harris Center for Infant and Toddler Development at the University of Minnesota and a statistician on the Minnesota Longitudinal Study of Parents and Children. In addition to research publications on the impact of adversity in early childhood development, she has written numerous articles including several for the Journal of ZERO TO THREE. Terrie lives in Minneapolis with her husband, Larry, and they are the proud and committed parents of three young adults. She can be reached on her blog at www.drterrierose.com or at terrie@babyspace.org.

REFERENCES

Agrawal, H. R., Gunderson, J., Holmes, B. M., & Lyons-Ruth, K. (2004). Attachment studies with borderline patients: A review. *Harvard Review of Psychiatry, 12*(2), 94-104.

Ainsworth, M. D. S. (1967). *Infancy in Uganda: Infant care and the growth of love.* Baltimore: Johns Hopkins.

American Academy of Pediatrics Committee on Environmental Health (2005). Lead exposure in children: Prevention, detection and management. *Pediatrics, 116*(4), 1036-1046.

Boekelheide, K., Blumberg, B., Chapin, R.E., Cote, I., Graziano, J.H. Janesick, A., ... & Myatt, L. (2012). Predicting later-life outcomes of early-life exposures. *Environmental Health Perspectives, 120*(10), 1353-1361.

Bowlby, J. (1969). *Attachment and loss: Attachment* (Vol. I). London: Hogarth.

Bowlby, J. (1999) [1982]. *Attachment and loss: Attachment* (Vol. I, 2nd ed.). New York: Basic Books.

Bowlby, J. (1988). *A secure base: Clinical applications of attachment theory.* London: Routledge.

Bowman, B. (2007). The effects of culture on thinking. *Exchange-Exchange Press, 175,* 12 15.

Brazelton, T.B. (1992). *Touchpoints: The essential reference-Your child's emotional and behavioral development.* New York: Addison-Wesley.

Breedlove, G., & Fryzelka, D. (2011). Depression screening during pregnancy. *Journal of Midwifery & Women's Health, 56*(1), 18-25.

Brennan, P. A., Pargas, R., Walker, E. F., Green, P., Jeffrey Newport, D., & Stowe, Z. (2008). Maternal depression and infant cortisol: Influences of timing, comorbidity and treatment. *Journal of Child Psychology and Psychiatry, 49*(10), 1099-1107.

Brooks-Gunn, J., & Markman, L. (2005). The contribution of parenting to ethnic and racial gaps in school readiness. *The Future of Children, 15*(1), 139-168.

Browne, J.V. (2003). New perspectives on premature infants and their parents. *Zero to Three, 24*(2), 4-12.

Buss, C., Davis, E. P., Hobel, C. J., & Sandman, C. A. (2011). Maternal pregnancy-specific anxiety is associated with child executive function at 6-9 years age. *Stress, 14*(6), 665-676.

Calonge, N., Petitti, D. B., DeWitt, T. G., Dietrich, A. J., Gregory, K. D., Grossman, D., ... & Wilt, T. (2009). Folic acid for the prevention of neural tube defects: US Preventive Services Task Force recommendation statement. *Annals of Internal Medicine, 150*(9), 626-631.

Carlson, E. A. (1998). A prospective longitudinal study of attachment disorganization/ disorientation. *Child development, 69*(4), 1107-1128.

Carter, A.S., Garrity-Rokous, E., Chazan-Cohen, R., Little, C., & Briggs-Gowan, M.J. (2001). Maternal depression and comorbidity: Predicting early parenting, attachment security, and toddler social-emotional problems and competencies. *Journal of the American Academy of Child & Adolescent Psychiatry, 40*(1)18 -26.

Cassidy, J., & Shaver, P. (Eds). (2008). *Handbook of attachment: Theory, research and clinical applications (2nd Ed.).* New York: Guilford Press.

Centers for Disease Control and Prevention. (2007) Pregnant? Don't Smoke!. Retrieved from http://www.cdc.gov/Features/PregnantDontSmoke/

Centers for Disease Control and Prevention (2008). Update on overall prevalence of major birth defects - Atlanta, Georgia, 1978-2005. Retrieved from http://www.cdc.gov/mmwr/preview/mmwrhtml/mm5701a2.htm

Centers for Disease Control and Prevention. (2009). *Intimate partner violence during pregnancy: A guide for clinicians* (PowerPoint presentation). Retrieved from http://www.cdc.gov/reproductivehealth/violence/IntimatePartnerViolence/index.htm

Centers for Disease Control and Prevention. (2010). Alcohol use in pregnancy. Retrieved from http://www.cdc.gov/ncbddd/fasd/alcohol-use.html

Chaddha, R. (2007). *Tale of two mice* (PowerPoint presentation). Retrieved from http://www.pbs.org/wgbh/nova/body/epigenetic-mice.html

Cicchetti, D., & Toth, S. L. (2000). Child maltreatment in the early years of life. In J. D. Osofsky & H. E. Fitzgerald (Eds.), *WAIMH Handbook of infant mental health* (Vol.4, pp. 257-294). New York: John Wiley & Sons.

Clarke-Stewart, K. A., Vandell, D. L., Burchinal, M., O'Brien, M., & McCartney, K. (2002). Do regulable features of child-care homes affect children's development? *Early Childhood Research Quarterly, 17*(1), 52-86.

Cohen, J., Cole, P., & Szrom, J (2011). A call to action on behalf of maltreated infants and toddlers. *American Humane Association, Center for the Study of Social Policy, Child Welfare League of America, Children's Defense Fund, and ZERO TO THREE.* Retrieved from http://www.childrensdefense.org/child-research-data-publications/data/call-to-action-on-behalf-of-maltreated-infants-and-toddlers.pdf

Cookson, H., Granell, R., Joinson, C., Ben-Shlomo, Y., & Henderson, A. J. (2009). Mothers' anxiety during pregnancy is associated with asthma in their children. *The Journal of Allergy and Clinical Immunology, 123*(4), 847.

Courchesne, E., Pierce, K., Schumann, C. M., Redcay, E., Buckwalter, J. A., Kennedy, D. P., & Morgan, J. (2007). Mapping early brain development in autism. *Neuron, 56*(2), 399-413.

Crews, D., Gore, A.C., Hsu, T.S., Dangleben, N.L., Spinetta, M., Schallert, T., … & Skinner, M.K. (2007). Transgenerational epigenetic imprints on mate preference. *Proceedings from the National Academy of Sciences, 104*(14) 5942-5946.

Davis, R.N., Davis, M.M., Freed, G.L., & Clark, S.J. (2011). Fathers' depression related to positive and negative parenting behaviors with 1-year old children. *Pediatrics, 127*(4), 612-618.

Dawson, G., Ashman, S. B., Panagiotides, Hessl, D., Self, J., Yamada, E., & Embry, L. (2003). Preschool outcomes of children of depressed mothers: Role of maternal behavior, contextual risk, and children's brain activity. *Child Development, 74*(4), 1158-1175.

Dawson, G., Frey, K., Self, J., Panagiotides, H., Hessl, D., Yamada, E., & Rinaldi, J. (1999). Frontal brain electrical activity in infants of depressed and nondepressed mothers: Relation to variations in infant behavior. *Development and Psychopathology, 11*(3), 589-605.

Day, N.L., Leech, S.L., Goldschmidt, L. (2011). The effects of prenatal marijuana exposure on delinquent behaviors are mediated by measures of neurocognitive functioning. *Neurotoxicology and Teratology, 33*(1), 129-136.

DeCasper, A. J., Lecanuet, J. P., Busnel, M. C., Granier-Deferre, C., & Maugeais, R. (1994). Fetal reactions to recurrent maternal speech. *Infant Behavior and Development, 17*(2), 159-164.

Diego, M. A., Field, T., Hernandez-Reif, M., Schanberg, S., Kuhn, C., & Gonzalez-Quintero, V. H. (2009). Prenatal depression restricts fetal growth. *Early Human Development, 85*(1), 65-70.

Dietz, D. M., LaPlant, Q., Watts, E. L., Hodes, G. E., Russo, S. J., Feng, J., ... & Nestler, E. J. (2011). Paternal transmission of stress-induced pathologies. *Biological Psychiatry, 70*(5), 408-414.

Doherty, W. J. (1999). *The intentional family: Simple rituals to strengthen family ties.* Avon Books.

Egeland, B., & Kreutzer, T., (1991). A longitudinal study of the effects of maternal stress and protective factors on the development of high risk children. In E.M. Cummings, A.L. Greend, & K. H. Karraker (Eds). *Life span developmental psychology: Perspectives on stress and coping.* Hillsdale, NJ: Erlbaum.

Engel, S. M., Berkowitz, G. S., Wolff, M. S., & Yehuda, R. (2005). Psychological trauma associated with the World Trade Center attacks and its effect on pregnancy outcome. *Pediatric Perinatal Epidemiology,* 19(5), 334-341.

Engel, S. M., Wetmur, J., Chen, J., Zhu, C., Barr, D. B., Canfield, R. L., & Wolff, M. S. (2011). Prenatal exposure to organophosphates, paraoxonase 1, and cognitive development in childhood. *Environmental Health Perspectives, 119*(8), 1182-1188.

Environmental Protection Agency. (2012). South Minneapolis Residential Soil Contamination Site. Retrieved from http://www.epa.gov/region5/cleanup/cmcheartland/

Ethen, M.K., Ramadhani, T.A., Scheuerle, A.E., Canfield, M.A., Wyszynski, D.F., Druschel, C.M., & Romitti, P.A. (2009). Alcohol consumption by women before and during pregnancy. *Journal of Maternal and Child Health, 13*(2), 274-285.

Feldman, H.S., Jones, K.L., Lindsay, S., Slymen, D., Klonoff-Cohen, H., Kao, K., ... & Chambers, C. (2012). Prenatal alcohol exposure patterns and alcohol-related birth defects and growth deficiencies: A prospective study. *Alcoholism: Clinical and Experimental Research, 36*(4), 670-676.

Field, T. (1995). Infants of depressed mothers. *Infant Behavior and Development, 18,* 1-13.

Field, T., Diego, M., & Hernadez-Reif, M. (2006). Prenatal depression effects on the fetus and newborn: A review. *Infant Behavior and Development, 29*(3), 445-455.

Fonagy, P., Target, M., & Gergely, G. (2000). Attachment and borderline personality disorder. A theory and some evidence. *The Psychiatric Clinics of North America, 23*(1), 103.

Fox, S. E., Levitt, P., & Nelson III, C. A. (2010). How the timing and quality of early experiences influence the development of brain architecture. *Child development, 81*(1), 28-40.

Francks, C., Maegawa, S., Laurén, J., Abrahams, B. S., Velayos-Baeza, A., Medland, S. E., ... & Monaco, A. P. (2007). LRRTM1 on chromosome 2p12 is a maternally suppressed gene that is associated paternally with handedness and schizophrenia. *Molecular Psychiatry, 12*(12), 1129-1139.

Gardner, J., & Harmon, T. (2002). Exploring resilience from a parent's perspective: A qualitative study of six resilient mothers of children with an intellectual disability. *Australian Social Work, 55*(1), 60-68.

Ghosh, J. K. C., Wilhelm, M. H., Dunkel-Schetter, C., Lombardi, C. A., & Ritz, B. R. (2010). Paternal support and preterm birth, and the moderation of effects of chronic stress: A study in Los Angeles County mothers. *Archives of Women's Mental Health, 13*(4), 327-338.

Goodman, J.H. (2004). Paternal postpartum depression, its relationship to maternal postpartum depression, and implications for family health. *Journal of Advanced Nursing, 45*(1), 26-35.

Grason, M.A., & Misra, D.P. (2009). Reducing exposure to environmental toxicants before birth: Moving from risk perception to risk reduction. *Public Health Reports, 124*(5), 629-641.

Greenspan, S.I., & Lewis, N.B. (1999). *Building healthy minds: The six experiences that create intelligence and emotional growth in babies and young children.* New York: Perseus.

Grote, N.K., Bridge, J.A., Gavin, A.R., Melville, J.L., Iyengar, S., & Katon, W.J. (2010). A meta-analysis of depression during pregnancy and the risk of preterm birth, low birth weight, and intrauterine growth restriction. *Archive of General Psychiatry, 67*(10), 1012-1024.

Gunnar, M.R., Bodersen, L., Nachmias, M., Buss, K. and Rigatuso, J. (1996). Stress reactivity and attachment security. *Developmental Psychobiology, 29*(3), 191-204.

Gunnar, M.R., Herrera, A., Hostinar, C.E. (2009). Stress and early brain development. In R. E. Tremblay, R. G. Barr, R. D. Peters, & M. Boivin

M (Eds.). *Encyclopedia on Early Childhood Development* [online] (pp. 1-8). Montreal, Quebec: Centre of Excellence for Early Childhood Development. Retrieved from http://www.child-encyclopedia.com/documents/Gunnar-Herrera-HostinarANGxp.pdf.

Gunnar, M. R., Kryzer, E., Van Ryzin, M. J., & Phillips, D. A. (2010). The rise in cortisol in family day care: Associations with aspects of care quality, child behavior, and child sex. *Child Development, 81*(3), 851-869.

Häberling, I.S., Badzakova-Trajkov, G., & Corballis, M.C. (2013). Asymmetries of the arcuate fasciculus in monozygotic twins: Genetic and nongenetic influences. *PLoS one, 8*(1), e52315. Retrieved from http://www.plosone.org/article/info:doi/10.1371/journal.pone.0052315.

Hazan, C., & Shaver, P. (1987). Romantic love conceptualized as an attachment process. *Journal of Personality and Social Psychology, 52*(3), 511-524.

Hennepin County & Omniciye Program (2009). Coming together for a common purpose: A collaborative evaluation between Hennepin County Research, Planning & Development Department and the Omniciye Program. Retrieved from http://www.hennepin.us/files/HennepinUS/Research%20Planning%20and%20Development/Research/OMNICIYE_ProgramYearOneEvaluationFindings.pdf

Isaacs, J. B. (2012). Starting school at a disadvantage: The school readiness of poor children. The social genome project. *Center on Children and Families at Brookings*.

Jablonka, E., & Lamb, M.J. (1995). *Epigenetic inheritance and evolution: The Lamarckian dimension.* New York: Oxford Press.

Johnston, D. W., Nicholls, M. E., Shah, M., & Shields, M. A. (2009). Nature's experiment? Handedness and early childhood development. *Demography, 46*(2), 281-301.

Jones, N.A., McFall, B.A., & Diego, M.A. (2004). Patterns of brain electrical activity in infants of depressed mothers who breastfeed and bottle feed: The mediating role in infant temperament. *Biological Psychology, 67*(1), 103-124.

Josefson, J. L., Hoffmann, J. A., & Metzger, B. E. (2013). Excessive weight gain in women with a normal pre-pregnancy BMI is associated with increased neonatal adiposity. *Pediatric obesity, 8*(2), e33-e36.

Joseph, R. (2000). Fetal brain behavior and cognitive development. *Developmental Review, 20*(1), 81-98.

Kessler, R. C., Chiu, W. T., Demler, O., & Walters, E. E. (2005). Prevalence, severity, and comorbidity of 12-month DSM-IV disorders in the National Comorbidity Survey Replication. *Archives of general psychiatry, 62*(6), 617.

Kaati, G., Bygren, L.O., & Edvinsson, S. (2002). Cardiovascular and diabetes mortality determined by nutrition during parents' and grandparents' slow growth period. *European Journal of Human Genetics, 10*(11), 682-688.

Kuhl, P. K. (2004). Early language acquisition: Cracking the speech code. *Nature Reviews Neuroscience, 5*(11), 831-843.

Kvalevaag, A. L., Ramchandani, P. G., Hove, O., Assmus, J., Eberhard-Gran, M., & Biringer, E. (2013). Paternal mental health and socioemotional and behavioral development in their children. *Pediatrics, 131*(2), e463-e469.

Ladefoged, P. (2001). Vowels and consonants: An introduction to the sounds of languages, Blackwells.

LaGasse, L. L., Derauf, C., Smith, L. M., Newman, E., Shah, R., Neal, C., & Lester, B. M. (2012). Prenatal methamphetamine exposure and childhood behavior problems at 3 and 5 years of age. *Pediatrics, 129*(4), 681-688.

Laplante, D. P., Barr, R. G., Brunet, A., Du Fort, G. G., Meaney, M. L., Saucier, J. F., & King, S. (2004). Stress during pregnancy affects general intellectual and language functioning in human toddlers. *Pediatric Research, 56*(3), 400-410.

Laurent, H.K., Leve, L.D., Neiderhiser, J.M., Shaw, D. S., Harold, G.T., & Reiss, D. (2013). Effects of prenatal and postnatal parent depressive symptoms on adopted child HPA regulation: Independent and moderate influences. *Developmental Psychology, 49*(5), 876-886.

Leddy, M. A., Power, M. L., & Schulkin, J. (2008). The impact of maternal obesity on maternal and fetal health. *Reviews in Obstetrics and Gynecology, 1*(4), 170.

LeMoine, S., & Morgan, G. (2004). Do states require child care programs to educate children?: Report #3: Infant/toddler rules to assure early education and strong relationships. Retrieved from http://ecap.crc. illinois.edu/docs/cc-educate/report3.pdf

Lester, B. M., & Twomey, J.E. (2008). Treatment of substance abuse during pregnancy. *Women's Health, 4*(1), 67-77.

Leventhal, T., & Brooks-Gunn, J. (2000). The neighborhoods they live in: The effects of neighborhood residence upon child and adolescent outcomes. *Psychological Bulletin, 126*, 309-337.

Lewis, S. J., Zuccolo, L., Smith, G. D., Macleod, J., Rodriguez, S., Draper, E. S., & Gray, R. (2012). Fetal alcohol exposure and IQ at age 8: Evidence from a population-based birth-cohort study. *PloS one, 7*(11), e49407.

Liu, Y., McDermott, S., Lawson, A., & Aelion, A.M. (2010). The relationship between mental retardation and developmental delays in children and the levels of arsenic, mercury and lead in soil samples taken near their mother's residence during pregnancy. *International Journal of Hygiene and Environmental Health, 213*(2), 116-123.

Lu, L.H., Johnson, A., O'Hare, E.D., Bookheimer, S.Y., Smith, L.M., O'Connor, M.J., & Sowell, E.R. (2009). Effects of prenatal methamphetamine exposure on verbal memory revealed with functional magnetic resonance imaging. *Journal of Developmental Behavioral Pediatrics, 30*(3), 185-192.

Mahler, M.S., Pine, F., & Bergman, A. (1975). *The psychological birth of the human infant*. New York: Basic Books.

March of Dimes Foundation. (2012). March of Dimes 2012 premature birth report card. Retrieved from http://www.marchofdimes.com/peristats/pdflib/998/US.pdf

Martin, J. A., Hamilton, B. E., Sutton, P. D., Ventura, S. J., Menacker, F., Kirmeyer, S., & Munson, M. L. (2007). Births: Final data for 2005. *National Vital Statistics Reports, 56*(6), 1-103.

Mathews, T. J. (2007). Trends in spina bifida and anencephalus in the United States, 1991-2005. *Hyattsville, MD: National Center for Health Statistics.*

May, P.A., Gossage, J.P., Kalberg, W.O., Robinson, L.K., Buckey, D., Manning, M., & Hoyme, H.E. (2009). Prevalence and epidemiologic characteristics of FASD from various research methods with an emphasis on recent in-school studies. *Developmental Disabilities Research Review, 15*(3), 176-192.

McDonald, A. (2007). Prenatal development. *The DANA Guide to Brain Health.* Retrieved from http://www.dana.org/news/brainhealth/detail.aspx?id=10050

Miller, K. (2005). Evaluating the Strong Beginnings programs: Results from Hennepin County's investment in early childhood education program(2002-2004). Retrieved from http://www.hennepin.us/files/HennepinUS/Research%20Planning%20and%20Development/Projects%20and%20Initiatives/Files/StrongBeginningsEvaluation.pdf

Minnesota Children's Defense Fund. (2011). Zero to three research to policy project: Maternal depression and early childhood full report. Retrieved from http://www.cdf-mn.org/sites/default/files/CDF_Maternal_Depression_5.pdf

Minnesota Department of Health. (2009, January). Disparities in infant mortality. Retrieved from http://www.health.state.mn.us/divs/chs/infantmortality/infantmortality09.pdf

Molliver, M. E., Kostovic, I., & van der Loos, H. (1973). The development of synapses in cerebral cortex of the human fetus. *Brain Research, 50*(2), 403-407.

Moon, C., Lagercrantz, H., & Kuhl, P. K. (2013). Language experienced in utero affects vowel perception after birth: A two-country study. *Acta Paediatrica, 102*(2), 156-160.

Moos, M.K. (2002). Preconceptional health promotion: Opportunities abound. *Journal of Maternal and Child Health, 6*(2), 71- 73.

Mvundura M., Amendah D., Kavanagh P. L., Sprinz, P. G., Grosse, S. D. (2009). Health care utilization and expenditures for privately and publicly insured children with sickle cell disease in the United States. *Pediatric Blood & Cancer, 53*(4), 642-646.

Myslajek, C. (2009). Racial disparity of child poverty in Minnesota: The hidden consequence of incarceration. *Hubert H. Humphrey Institute of Public Affairs.*

National Research Council and Institute of Medicine. (2000). From neurons to neighborhoods: The science of early childhood development. Committee on Integrating the Science of Early Childhood Development. Jack P. Shonkoff and Deborah A. Phillips, eds. Board on Children, Youth, and Families, Commission on Behavioural and Social Sciences and Education. Washington, D.C.: National Academy

National Scientific Council on the Developing Child. (2007). The science of early childhood development. Retrieved from http://developingchild. harvard.edu/resources/reports_and_working_papers/science_of_early_childhood_development/

National Scientific Council on the Developing Child. (2008). Mental health problems in early childhood can impair learning and behavior for life: Working paper No. 6. Retrieved from www.developingchild.harvard. edu.

Nelson, C., Zeanah, C., Fox, N., Marshall, P., Smyke, A., & Guthrie, D. (2007). Cognitive recovery in socially deprived young children: The Bucharest early intervention project. *Science, 318*(5858), 1937-1940.

Nguyen, D., Smith, L.M., Lagasse, L.L., Derauf, C., Grant, P., Shah, R....Lester, B.M. (2010). Intrauterine growth of infants exposed to prenatal methamphetamines: Results from infant development, environment, and lifestyle study. *Journal of Pediatrics, 157*(2), 337-339.

NICHD Early Child Care Research Network. (2000). Characteristics and quality of child care for toddlers and preschoolers. *Applied Developmental Psychology, 4*(3), 116-135.

NICHD Early Child Care Research Network. (2006). Infant-mother attachment classification: Risk and protection in relation to changing maternal caregiving quality. *Developmental Psychology, 42*(1), 38-58.

Nosarti, C., Reichenberg, A., Murray, R. M., Cnattingius, S., Lambe, M. P., Yin, L., & Hultman, C. M. (2012). Preterm birth and psychiatric disorders in young adult life. *Archives of General Psychiatry, 69*(6), 610-617.

Oberlander, T. F., Papsdorf, M., Brain, U. M., Misri, S., Ross, C., and Grunau, R. E. (2010). Prenatal effects of selective serotonin reuptake inhibitor antidepressants, serotonin transporter promoter genotype (SLC6A4), and maternal mood on child behavior at 3 years of age. *Archives of Pediatrics & Adolescent Medicine, 164*(5), 444-451.

Oberlander, T.F., Weinber, J., Papsdorf, M., Grunau, R., Misri, S., Devline, A.M. (2008). Prenatal exposure to maternal depression, neonatal methylation of human glucocorticoid receptor gene (NR3C1) and infant cortisol response. *Epigenetics 3*(2), 97-106.

O'Connor, T.G., Heron, J., Glover, V., & Alspac Study Team. (2002). Antenatal anxiety predicts child behavioral/emotional problems independently of postnatal depression. *Journal of American Academy of Child and Adolescent Psychiatry, 41*(12), 1470-1477.

Parker, S.W. & Nelson, C.A. (2005). The impact of early institutional rearing on the ability to discriminate facial expressions of emotions: An event-related potential study. *Child Development, 76*(1), 54-72.

Parlakian, R., & Seibel, N. L. (2002). *Building Strong Foundations: Practical Guidance for Promoting the Social-Emotional Development of Infants and Toddlers.* Zero to Three, 2000 M Street, NW, Suite 200, Washington, DC 20036-3307.

Paulson, J.F., & Bazemore, S.D. (2010). Prenatal and postpartum depression in fathers and its association with maternal depression: A meta-analysis. *Journal of the American Medical Association, 303*(19), 1961-1969.

Paz, I., Gale, R., Laor, A., Danon, Y. L., Stevenson, D. K., & Seidman, D. S. (1995). The cognitive outcome of full-term small for gestational age infants at late adolescence. *Obstetrics & Gynecology, 85*(3), 452-456.

Pembrey, M. E., Bygren, L. O., Kaati, G., Edvinsson, S., Northstone, K., Sjöström, M., & Golding, J. (2005). Sex-specific, male-line transgenerational responses in humans. *European Journal of Human Genetics, 14*(2), 159-166.

Petitto, L. A., & Marentette, P. F. (1991). Babbling in the manual mode: Evidence for the ontogeny of language. *Science, 251*(5000), 1493-1496.

Pianta, R.C., Cox, M.J., & Snow, K.L. (2007). *School readiness and the transition to kindergarten in the era of accountability.* Baltimore: Brookes Publishing Company.

Pianta, R.C., Erickson, M.F., Wagner, N.C., Kreutzer, T., & Egeland, B. (1990). Early predictors of referral for special services: Child-based measures versus mother-child interactions. *School Psychological Review, 19*(2), 240-250.

Power, M. L., Cogswell, M. E., & Schulkin, J. (2006). Obesity prevention and treatment practices of U.S. obstetrician-gynecologists. *Obstetrics & Gynecology, 108*(4), 961-968.

Rabinowicz, T., de Courten-Myers, G. M., Petetot, J. M. C., Guohua, X. I., & de los Reyes, E. (1996). Human cortex development: Estimates of neuronal numbers indicate major loss late during gestation. *Journal of Neuropathology & Experimental Neurology, 55*(4), 320-328.

Rahman, A., Persson, L. A., Nermell, B., El Arifeen, S., Ekström, E. C., Smith, A. H., & Vahter, M. (2010). Arsenic exposure and risk of spontaneous abortion, stillbirth, and infant mortality. *Epidemiology, 21*(6), 797-804.

Ramanathan, S., Balasubramanian, N., & Krishnadas, R. (2013). Macroeconomic environment during infancy as a possible risk factor for adolescent behavioral problems. *JAMA Psychiatry, 70*(2), 218-225.

Ramchandani, P.G., Stein, A., O'Connor, T.G., Heron, J., Murray, L., & Evans, J. (2008). Depression in men in the postnatal period and later child psychopathology: A population cohort study. *Journal of the American Academy of Child and Adolescent Psychiatry, 47*(4), 390-398.

Reichman, N. E. (2005). Low birth weight and school readiness. *The Future of Children, 15*(1), 91-116.

Roben, C. K., Cole, P. M., & Armstrong, L. M. (2012). Longitudinal relations among language skills, anger expression, and regulatory strategies in early childhood. *Child Development, 0(0)*, 1-15.

Rolnick, A., & Grunewald, R. (2003). Early childhood development: Economic development with a high public return. *The Region, 17*(4), 6-12.

Rose, T. (2012a) Safeguarding young children: The role of child care. *The Early Report: Coordinating our systems of care to promote healthy development in young children.* Oct, 21-22.

Rose, T. (2012b). School readiness is more than ABCs and 123s. *Journal of ZERO TO THREE, 33*(1),17-23.

Rose, T. (2007). Integrating mental health in early education settings. *Minnesota Head Start Association Inc.*, Duluth, Minnesota.

Ruchat, S. M., & Mottola, M. F. (2012). Preventing long-term risk of obesity for two generations: Prenatal physical activity is part of the puzzle. *Journal of Pregnancy.*

Rutter, M., Sonuga-Barke, E.J., Beckett, C., Castle, J., Kreppner, J., Kumsta, R., ... & Gunnar, M.R. (2010). Deprivation-specific psychological patterns: Effects of institutional deprivation. *Monographs of the Society for Research in Child Development, 75*(1), 1-252.

Scerri, T. S., Brandler, W. M., Paracchini, S., Morris, A. P., Ring, S. M., Richardson, A. J., & Monaco, A. P. (2011). PCSK6 is associated with handedness in individuals with dyslexia. *Human Molecular Genetics, 20*(3), 608-614.

Schneider, M. L., Moore, C. F., Gajewski, L. L., Larson, J. A., Roberts, A. D., Converse, A. K., DeJesus, O. T. (2008). Sensory processing disorder in a primate model: evidence from a longitudinal study of prenatal alcohol and prenatal stress effects. *Child Development, 79*(1), 100-113.

Schipper, J., IJzendoorn, M. H. V., & Tavecchio, L. W. (2004). Stability in center day care: Relations with children's well-being and problem behavior in day care. *Social Development, 13*(4), 531-550.

Schore, A. N. (2001). Effects of a secure attachment relationship on right brain development, affect regulation, and infant mental health. *Infant Mental Health Journal, 22*(1-2), 7-66.

Shonkoff, J.P., Garner, A.S., Seigel, B.S., Dobbins, M.I., Earls, M.F., Garner, A.S., ... Wood, D.L. (2012). The lifelong effects of early childhood adversity and toxic stress. *Pediatrics, 129*(1), e232-e246. Retrieved from: http://pediatrics.aappublications.org/content/129/1/e232.full.html

Shonkoff, J. P., & Phillips, D. A. (Eds.). (2000). *From neurons to neighborhoods: The science of early childhood development.* National Academies Press.

Singh, A. V., Knudsen, T. B., Rouchka, E. C., Ngalame, N. O., Arteel, G. E., Piao, Y., & Ko, M. S. (2012). Prenatal arsenic exposure alters gene expression in the adult liver to a proinflammatory state contributing to accelerated atherosclerosis. *PloS one, 7*(6), e38713.

Skogerbø, Å., Kesmodel, U. S., Wimberley, T., Støvring, H., Bertrand, J., Landrø, N. I., & Mortensen, E. L. (2012). The effects of low to moderate alcohol consumption and binge drinking in early pregnancy on executive function in 5-year-old children. *BJOG: An International Journal of Obstetrics & Gynaecology, 119*(10), 1201-1210.

Sowell, E.R., Leow, A.D., Bookheimer, S.Y., Smith, L.M., O'Conner, M.J., Kan, E., ...Thompson, P.M. (2010). Differentiating prenatal exposure to methamphetamine and alcohol versus alcohol and not methamphetamine using tensor-based brain morphometry and discriminant analysis. *Journal of Neuroscience, 30*(11), 3876-3885.

Squires, J., Bicker, D., Heo, K., & Twombly, E. (2001). Identification of social-emotional problems in young children using a parent-completed screening measure. *Early Childhood Research Quarterly, 16*(4), 405-419.

Sroufe, L. A., Egeland, B., Carlson, E. A., & Collins, W. A. (2005). *The development of the person: The Minnesota study of risk and adaptation from birth to adulthood.* Guilford Publication.

Sroufe, L.A., Egeland, B., & Kreutzer, T. (1990). The fate of early experience following developmental change: Longitudinal approach to individual adaptation in childhood. *Child Development, 61*(5), 1363-1373.

Sroufe, L.A., & Fleeson, J. (1986). Attachment and the construction of relationships. In W. Hartup & Z. Rubin (Eds.), *Relationships and development* (pp. 51-71). Hillsdale, NJ: Erlbaum.

Streissguth, A., Bookstein, F., Barr, H., Sampson, P., O'malley, K., Young, J. (2004). Risk factors for adverse life outcomes in fetal alcohol syndrome and fetal alcohol effects. *Journal of Developmental Behavioral Pediatrics, 25*(4), 228-238.

Stephansson, O., Kieler, H., Haglund, B., Artama, M., Engeland, A., Furu, K., & Valdimarsdóttir, U. (2013). Selective serotonin reuptake inhibitors during pregnancy and risk of stillbirth and infant mortality. *Journal of the American Medical Association, 309*(1), 48-54.

Stotland, N. E., Gilbert, P., Bogetz, A., Harper, C. C., Abrams, B., & Gerbert, B. (2010). Preventing excessive weight gain in pregnancy: How do prenatal care providers approach counseling?. *Journal of Women's Health, 19*(4), 807-814.

Surén, P., Roth, C., Bresnahan, M., Haugen, M., Hornig, M., Hirtz, D., & Stoltenberg, C. (2013). Association between maternal use of folic acid supplements and risk of autism spectrum disorders in children. *Journal of the American Medical Association, 309*(6), 570-577.

Swain, J. E., Lorberbaum, J. P., Kose, S., & Strathearn, L. (2007). Brain basis of early parent–infant interactions: Psychology, physiology, and in vivo functional neuroimaging studies. *Journal of Child Psychology and Psychiatry, 48*(3-4), 262-287.

Syvertsen, A. K., Scales, P. C., Roehlkepartain, E., Benson, P. L., Fraher, K., Longfellow, S., & Reagan-Montiel, M. M. (2011). The American family assets study. SEARCH INSTITUTE. Retrieved from http://www.search-institute.org/system/files/American_Family_Assets_Study_Technical_Notes.pdf

Talge, N. M., Neal, C., & Glover, V. (2007). Antenatal maternal stress and long-term effects on child neurodevelopment: How and why?. *Journal of Child Psychology and Psychiatry, 48*(3-4), 245-261.

Tegethoff, M., Greene, N., Olsen, J., Schaffner, E., & Meinlschmidt, G. (2011). Stress during pregnancy and offspring pediatric disease: A national cohort study. *Environmental Health Perspectives, 119*(11), 1647.

Tierney, A. L., & Nelson III, C. A. (2009). Brain development and the role of experience in the early years. *Zero to Three, 30*(2), 9.

Titterton, M., Hill, M., & Smart, H. (2002). Mental health promotion and the early years: The evidence base: Risk protection and resilience. *Journal of Mental Health Promotion, 1*(1) 20–35.

Trevarthen, C., & Aitken, K. J. (1994). Brain development, infant communication, and empathy disorders: Intrinsic factors in child mental health. *Development and Psychopathology, 6*, 597-597.

Tronick, E. (2012). *The neurobehavioral and social-emotional development of infants and children.* New York: W. W. Norton & Company, Inc.

Troy, M., & Sroufe, L.A. (1987). Victimization among preschoolers: The role of attachment relationships history. *Journal of the American Academy of Child and Adolescent Psychiatry, 26*(2), 166-172.

Twomey, J., LaGasse, L., Derauf, C., Newman, E., Shar, R., Smith, L. ... & Lester, B. (2013). Prenatal methamphetamine exposure, home environment, and primary caregiver risk factors predict child behavioral problems at 5 years. *American Journal of Orthopsychiatry, 83*(1), 64-72.

U.S. Census Bureau. (n.d.). *American Community Survey 2006-2008.* Retrieved from http://www.census.gov/acs/www/

U.S. Department of Energy Genome Program. (2012). Retrieved from http://genomics.energy.gov.

U.S. Department of Health and Human Services. (2011). Healthy people 2020 – Improving the health of Americans. Retrieved from http://healthypeople.gov/2020/

U.S. Department of Health and Human Services. (2011b). Home visiting evidence of effectiveness: Child development and school readiness outcomes. Retrieved from http://homvee.acf.hhs.gov/document.aspx?rid=2&sid=3

U.S. Department of Health and Human Services, Health Resources and Services Administration, Maternal and Child Health Bureau (2011). *Child Health USA.* Rockville, Maryland: U.S. Department of Health and Human Services.

U.S. Department of Health and Human Services. (2012). 2012 Resource Guide: Preventing child maltreatment and promoting well-being: A network for action. Retrieved from http://www.childwelfare.gov/pubs/guide2012/guide.pdf

U.S. Preventive Services Task Force. (2009). Folic acid for the prevention of neural tube defects. Retrieved from http://www.uspreventiveservicestaskforce.org/uspstf09/folicacid/folicacidrs.htm

van IJzendoom, M. H., Schuengel, C., & Bakersman-Kranenburg, M. J. (in press). Disorganized attachment in early childhood: Meta-analysis of precursors, concomitants, and sequelae. *Development and Psychopathology.*

Vandell, D. L., Belsky, J., Burchinal, M., Steinberg, L., & Vandergrift, N. (2010). Do effects of early child care extend to age 15 years? Results from the NICHD study of early child care and youth development. *Child Development, 81*(3), 737-756.

Vaux, K., & Chambers, C. (2010). Fetal Alcohol Syndrome. Retrieved from http://emedicine.medscape.com/article/974016-overview

Watamura, S., Sebanc, A., Donzella, B., & Gunnar, M. (2002). Naptime at childcare: Effects on salivary cortisol levels. *Developmental Psychobiology, 40,* 33-42.

Watamura, S. E., Donzella, B., Kertes, D. A., & Gunnar, M. R. (2004). Developmental changes in baseline cortisol activity in early childhood: Relations with napping and effortful control. *Developmental Psychobiology, 45*(3), 125-133.

Waters, E., Wippman, J., & Sroufe, L.A. (1979). Attachment, positive affect, and competence in the peer group: Two studies in construct validation. *Child Development, 51,* 821-829.

Weinberg, M. K., & Tronick, E. Z. (1998). Emotional characteristics of infants associated with maternal depression and anxiety. *Pediatrics, 102*(Supplement E1), 1298-1304.

Werker, J. F., Pons, F., Dietrich, C., Kajikawa, S., Fais, L., & Amano, S. (2007). Infant-directed speech supports phonetic category learning in English and Japanese. *Cognition, 103*(1), 147-162.

Werner, E. E. (1990). Protective factors and individual resilience. *Handbook of early childhood intervention, 2,* 115-132.

Wessel, C. (2009). Poverty up, median income down, racial disparities persist. Retrieved from http://minnesotabudgetbites.org/2010/09/28/minnesota-poverty-up-median-income-down-racial-disparities-persist/

White, B. L., Kaban, B., Shapiro, B., & Attanucci, J. (1977). Competence and experience. In *The Structuring of Experience* (pp. 115-152). Springer US.

Williams, D., Rose, T., Gorman, L. A., Fitzgerald, H. E., Cozza, S. J., Lieberman, A. F., ... & Eggebeen, D. J. (2007). I say hello; you say good-bye: When babies are born while fathers are away. *Journal of ZERO TO THREE, 27*(6).

Wisner, K.L., Sit, D.K., McShea, M.C., Rizzo, D. M., Zoretich, R., Hughes, C.L., ... & Hanusa, B.H. (2013). Onset timing, thoughts of self-harm, and diagnoses in postpartum women with screen-positive depression findings. *Journal of the American Medical Association, Psychiatry 70*(5), 490-498.

Wolff, G.L., Kodell, R.L., Moore, S.R., & Cooney, C.A. (1998). Maternal epigenetics and methyl supplements affect agouti gene expression in Avy/a mice. *The Journal of the Federation of American Societies for Experimental Biology, 12*(10), 949-957.

Yonkers, K. A., Wisner, K. L., Stewart, D. E., Oberlander, T. F., Dell, D. L., Stotland, N., & Lockwood, C. (2009). The management of depression during pregnancy: A report from the American Psychiatric Association and the American College of Obstetricians and Gynecologists. *General Hospital Psychiatry, 31*(5), 403.

Zeanah, C. H., & Zeanah, P. D. (2001). Towards a definition of infant mental health. *Zero to Three, 22*(1), 13-20.

Zero to Three. (1994). *Diagnostic classification of mental health and developmental disorders of infancy and early childhood.* Washington, DC: ZERO TO THREE Press.

Zero to Three. (2005). *Diagnostic classification of mental health and developmental disorders of infancy and early childhood: Revised edition (DC: 0-3R).* Washington, DC: ZERO TO THREE Press.